Easy Coloring Book For Adults

An Adult Coloring Book of 40 Basic, Simple and Bold Mandalas for Beginners

Adult Coloring World

ISBN-13: 978-1522719786

ISBN-10: 1522719784

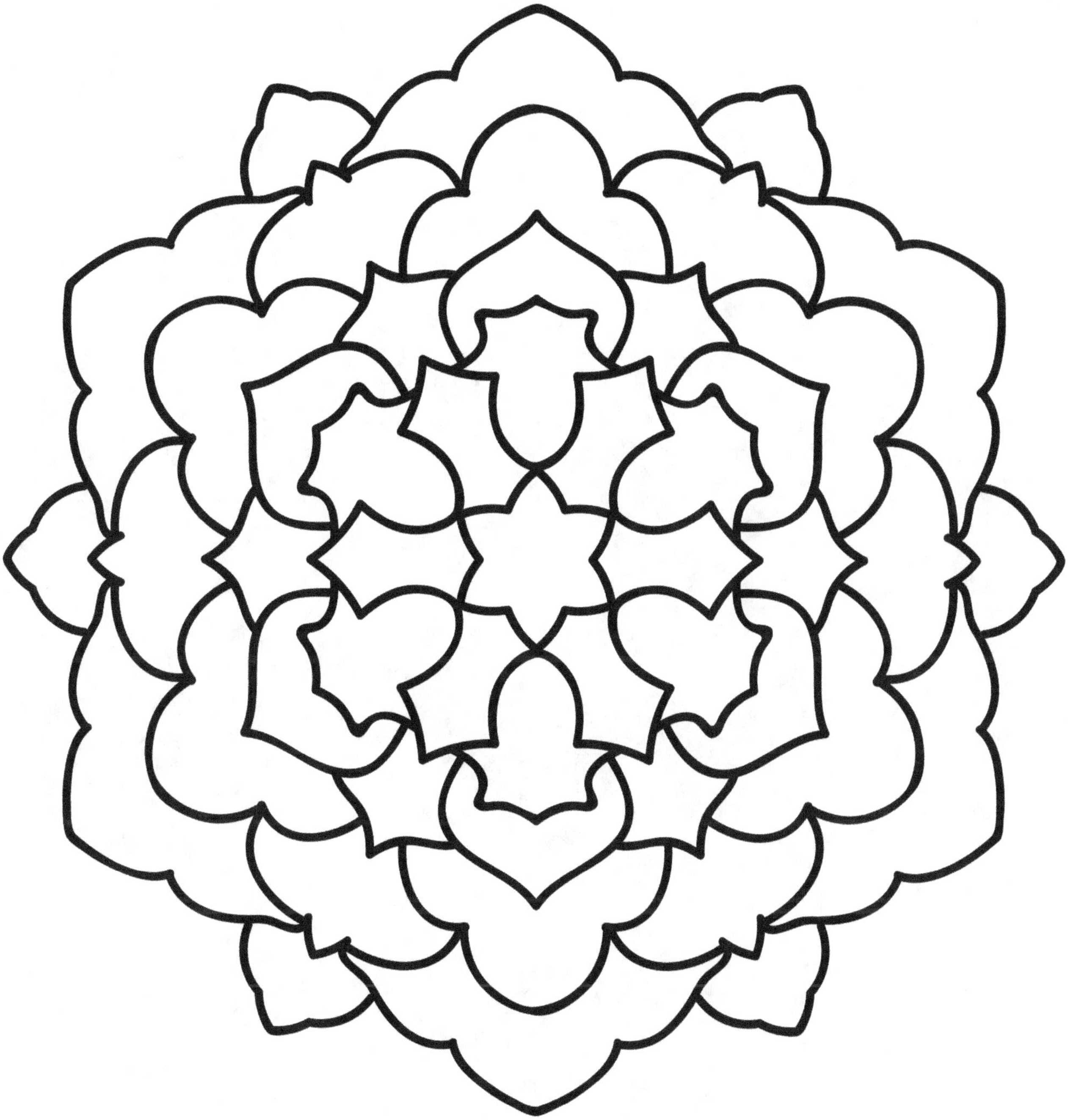

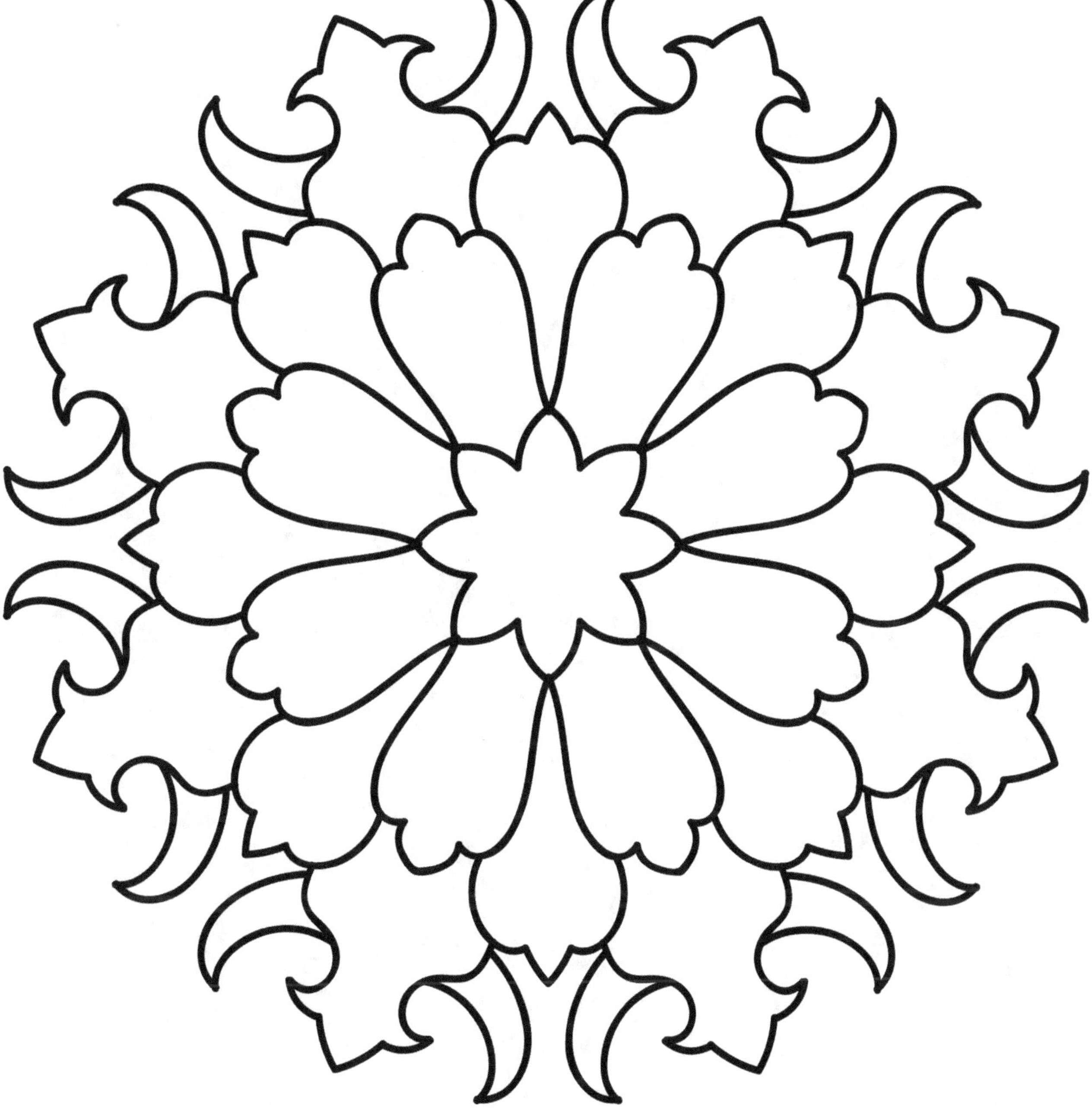

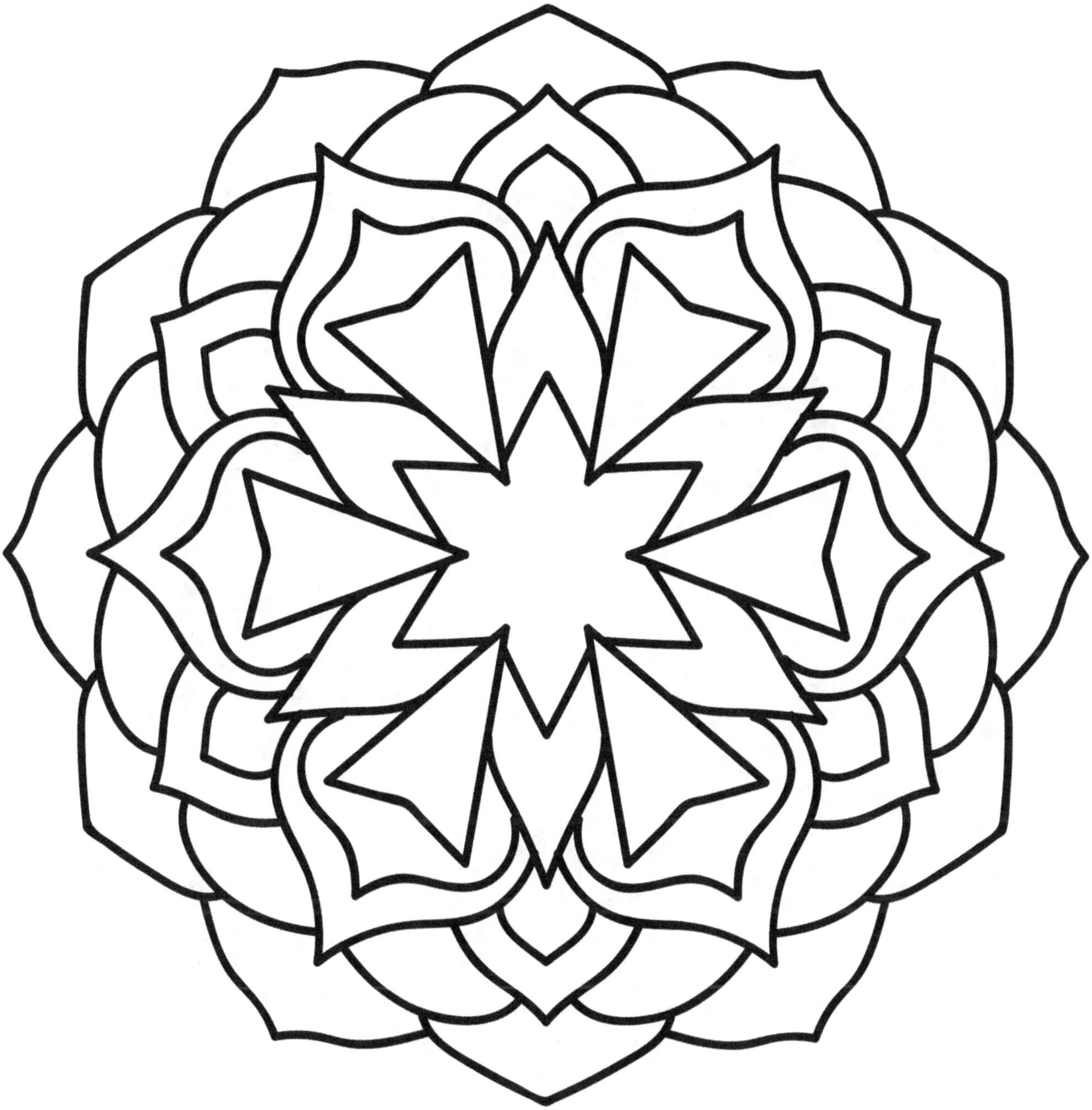

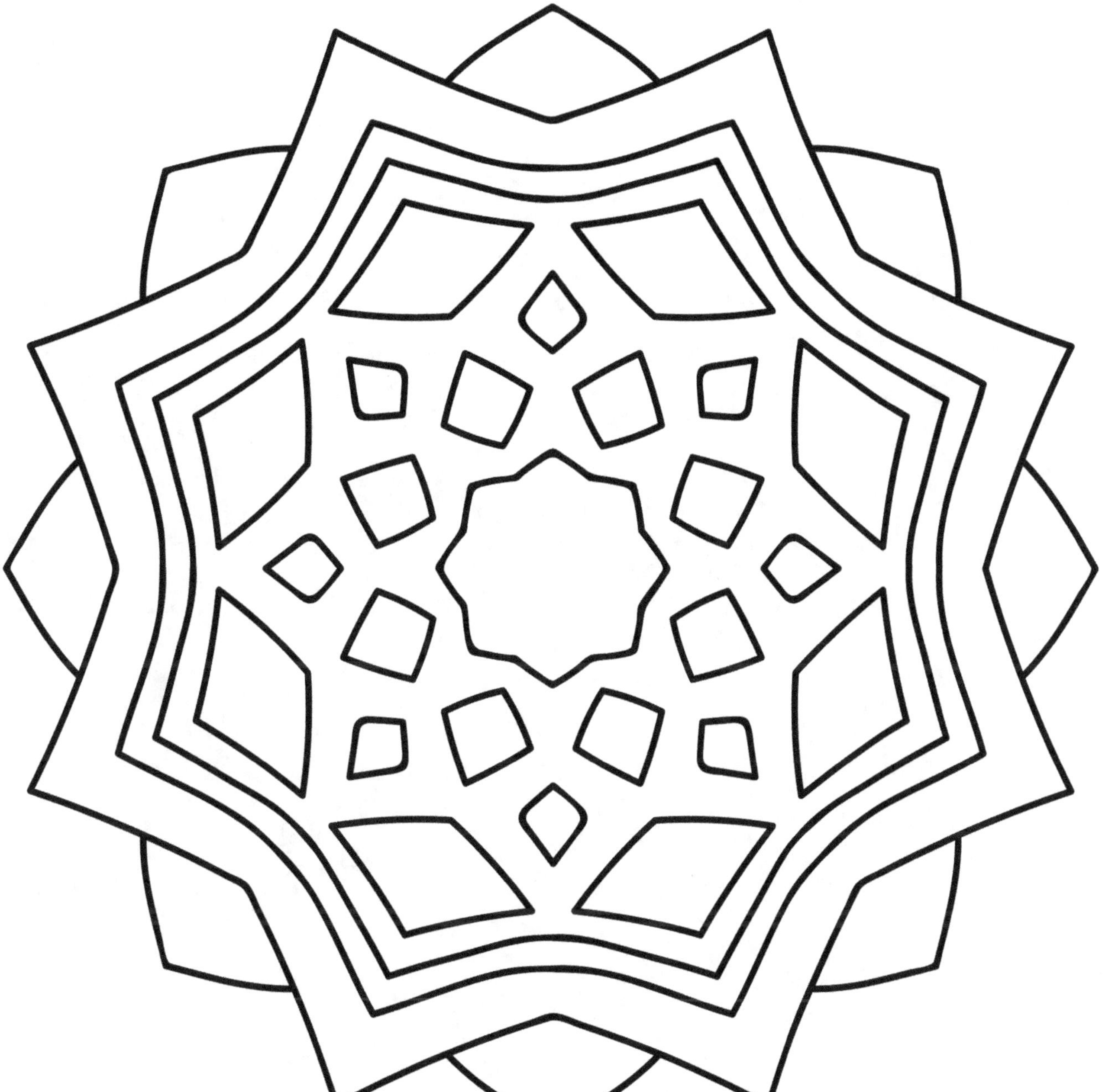

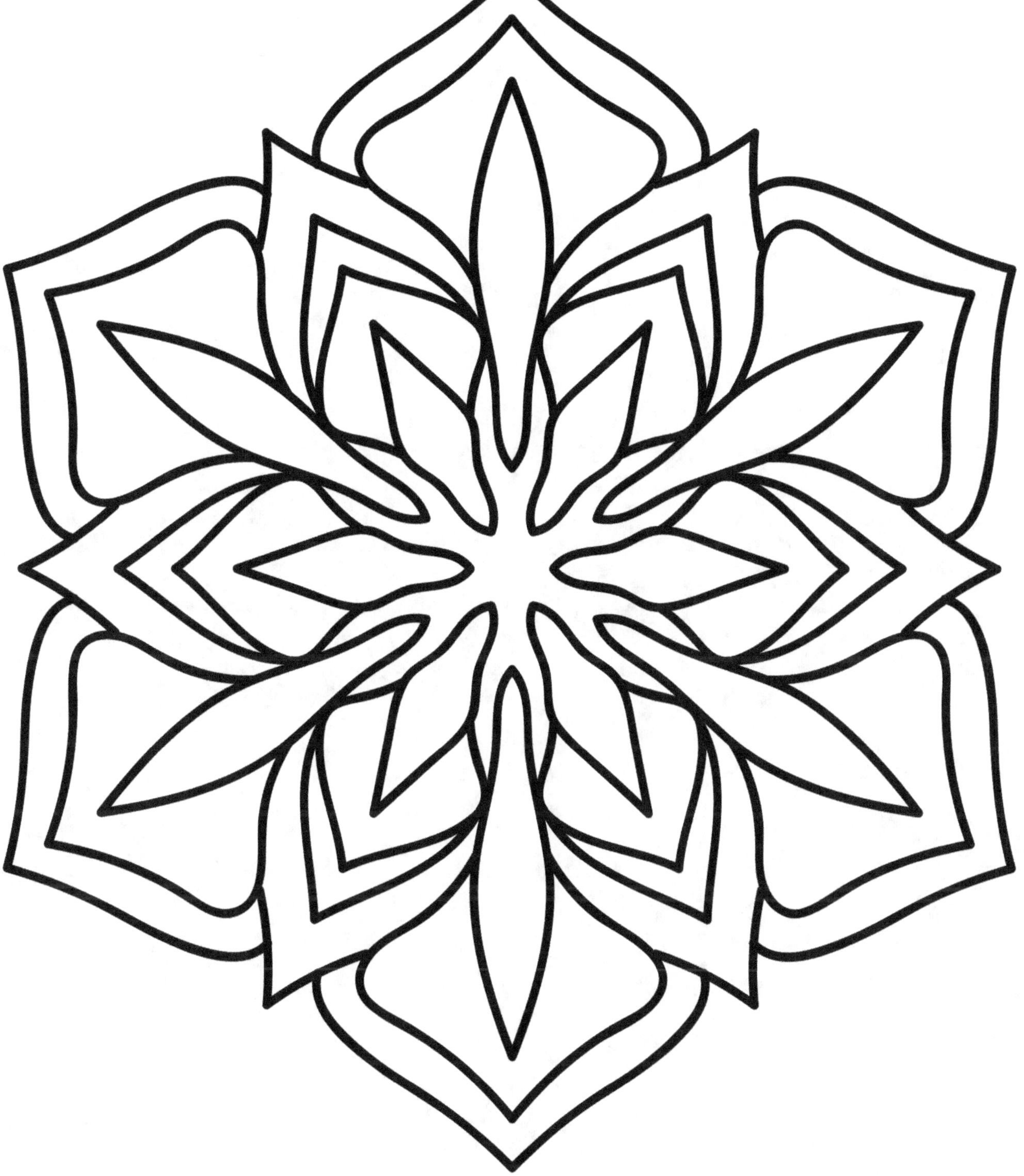

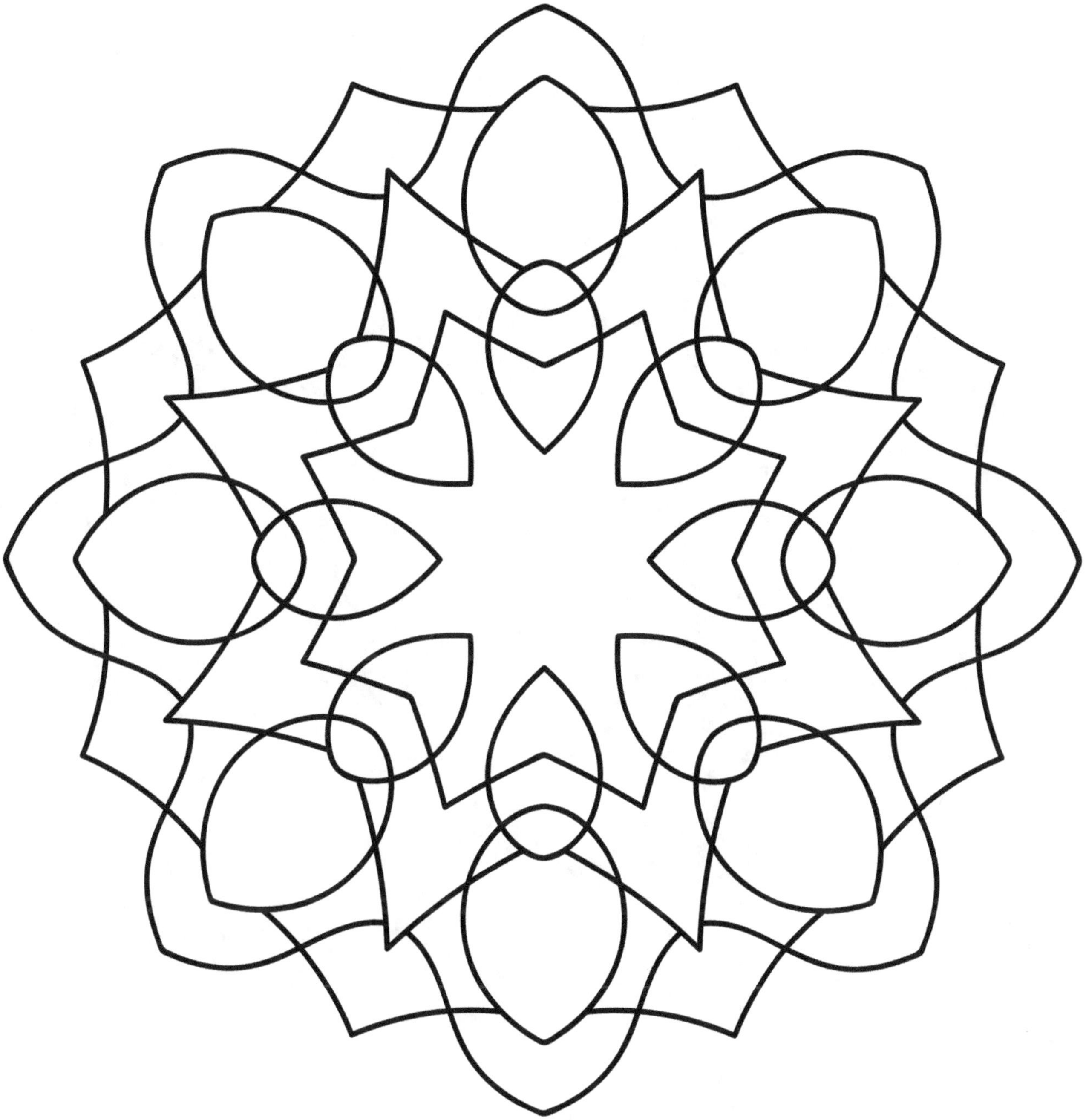

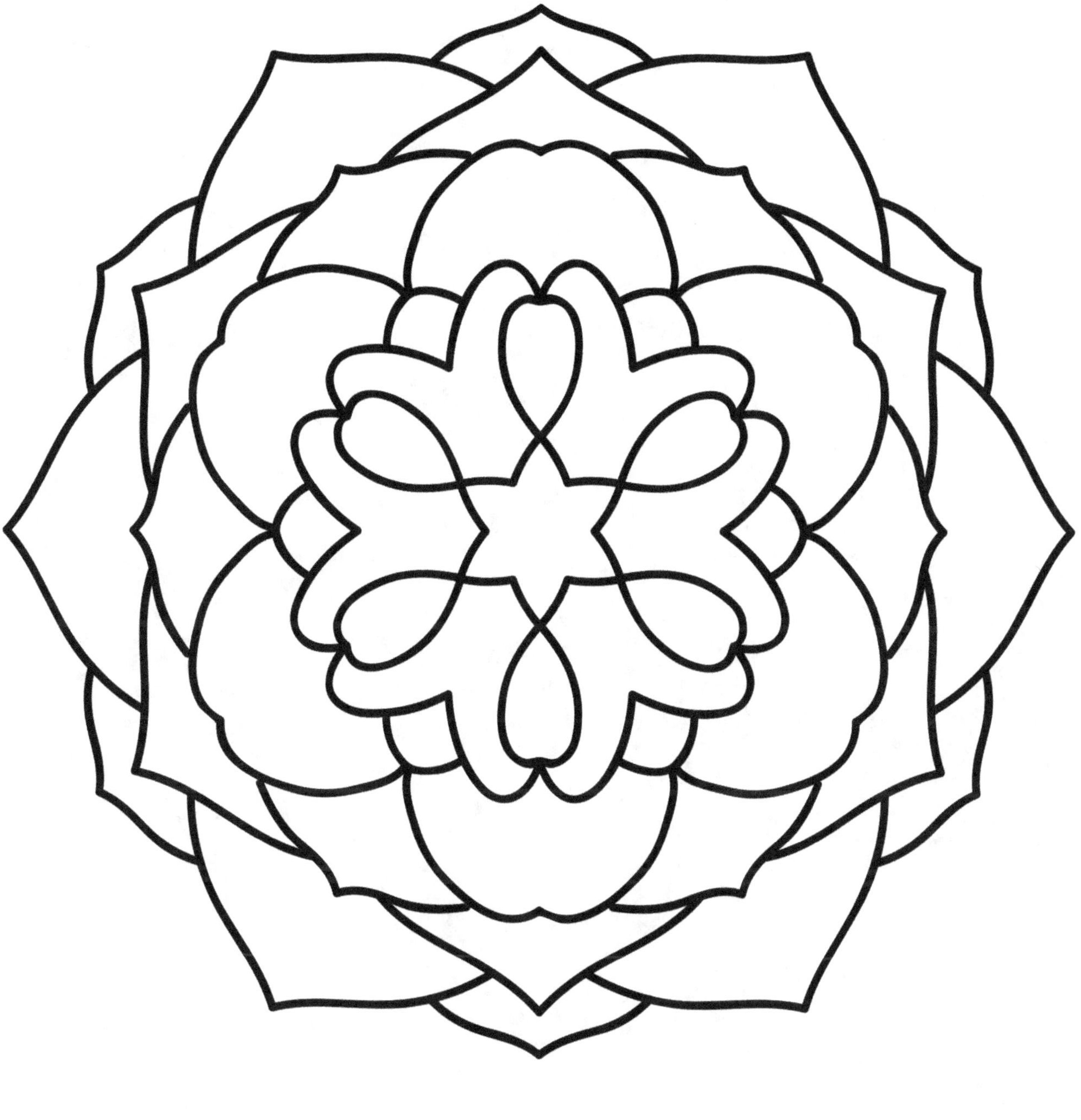

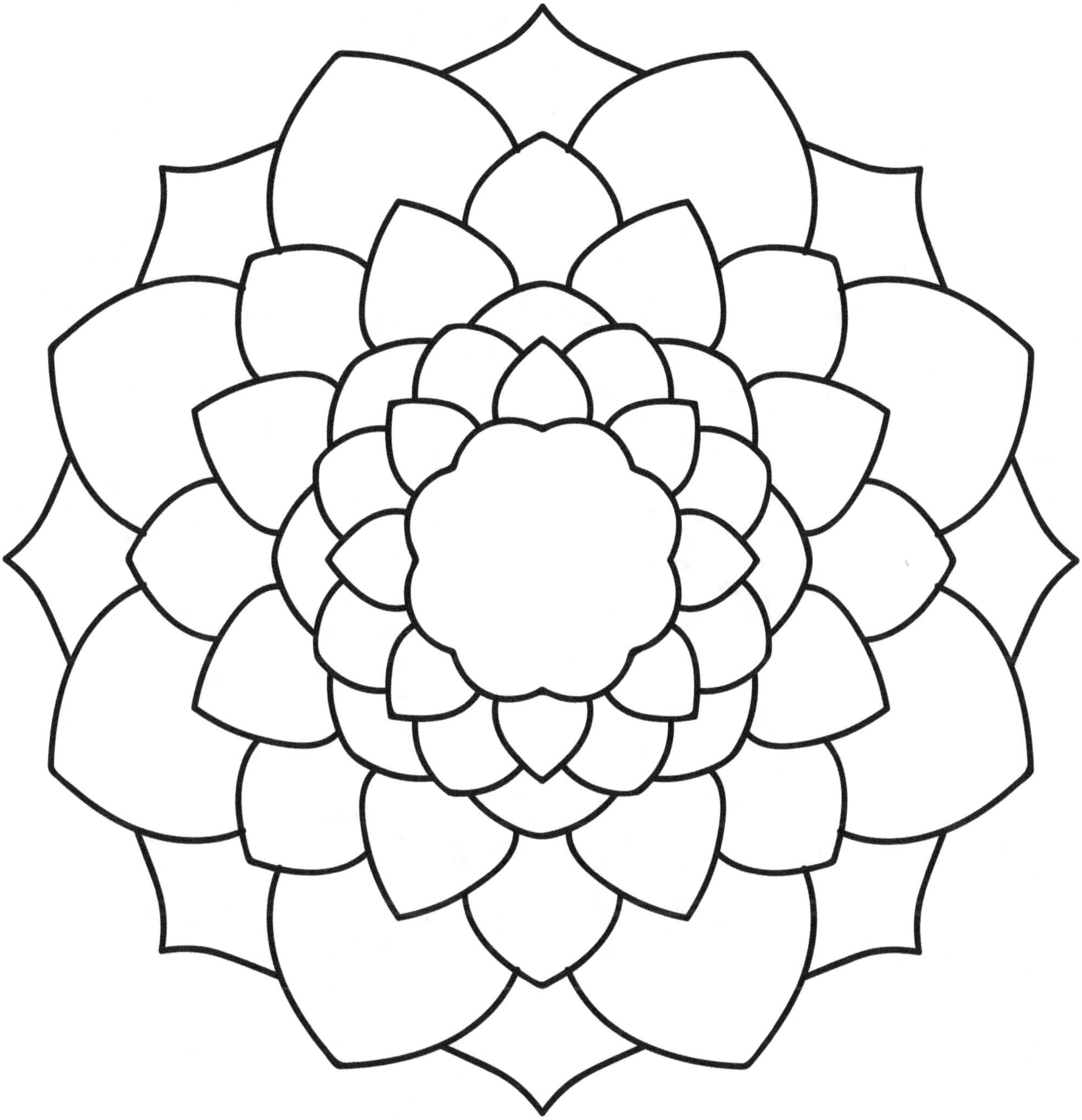

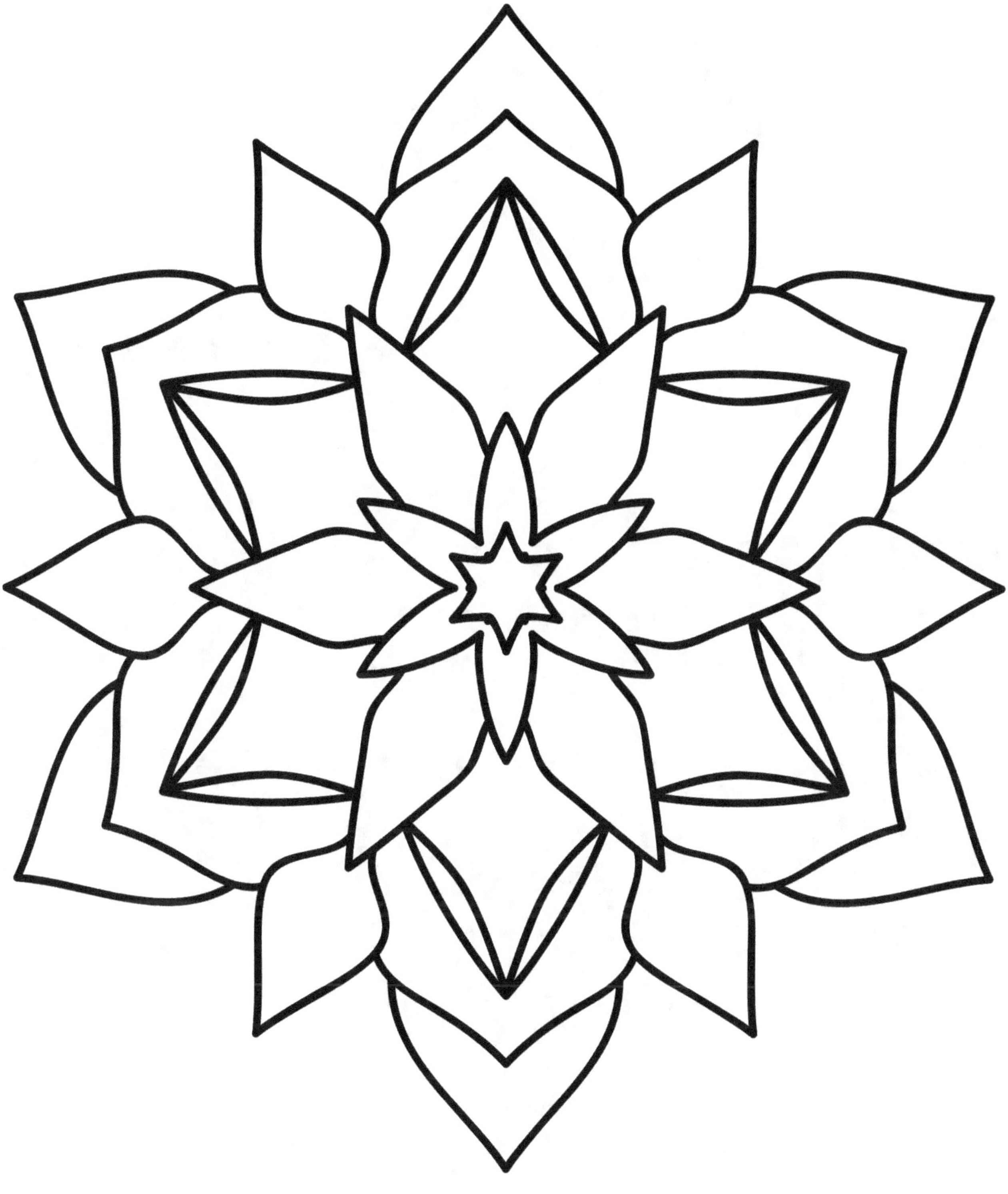

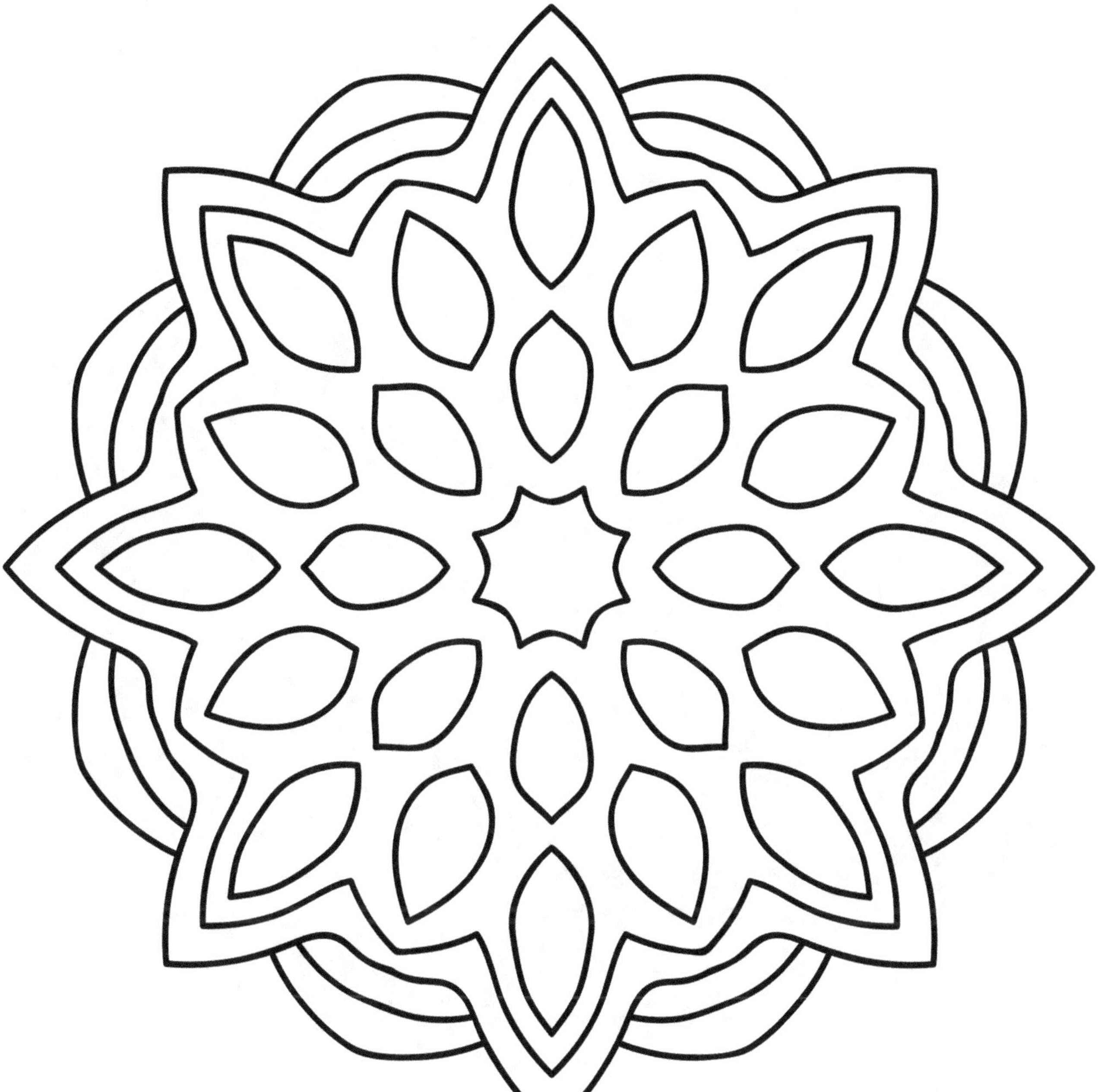

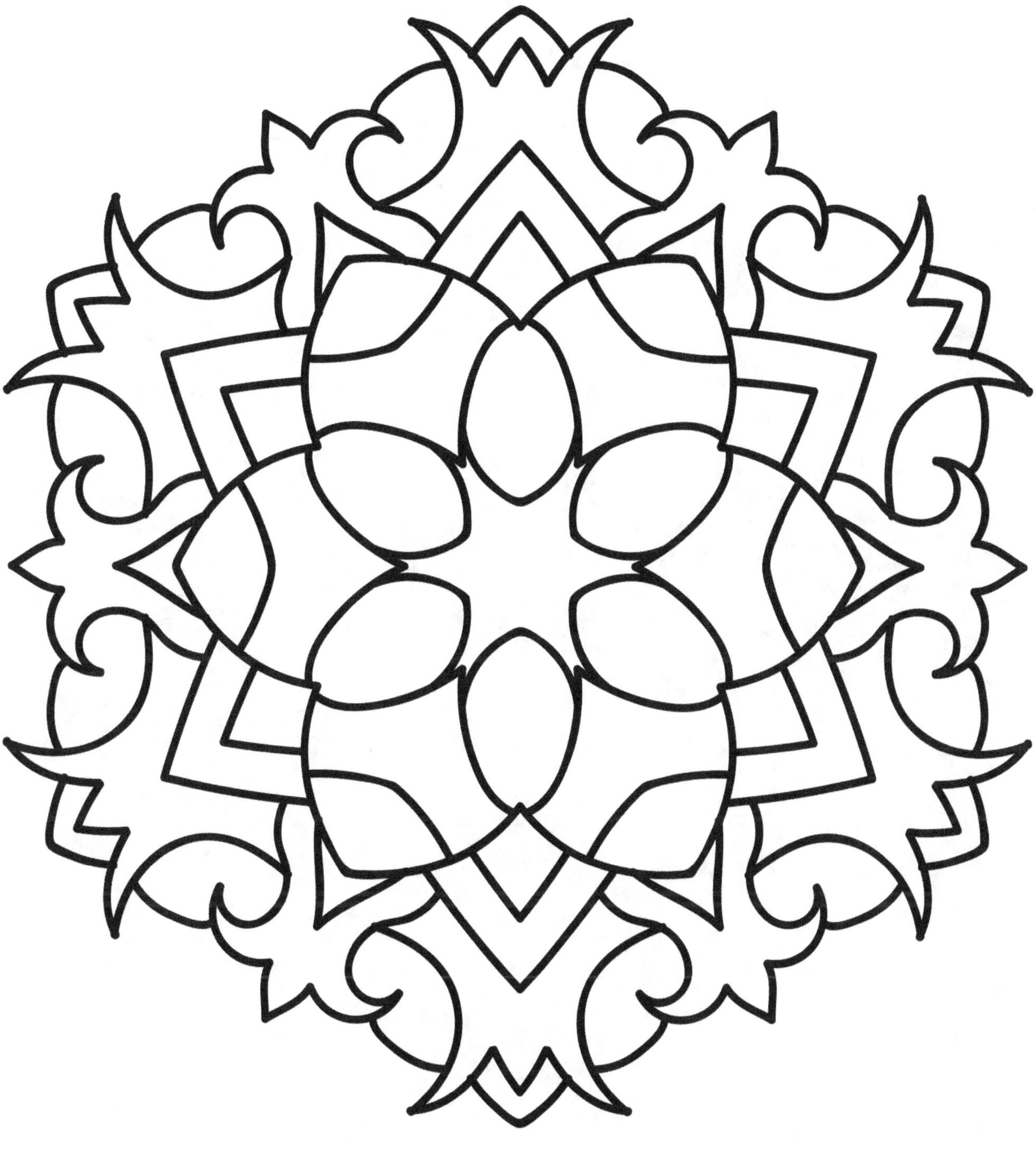

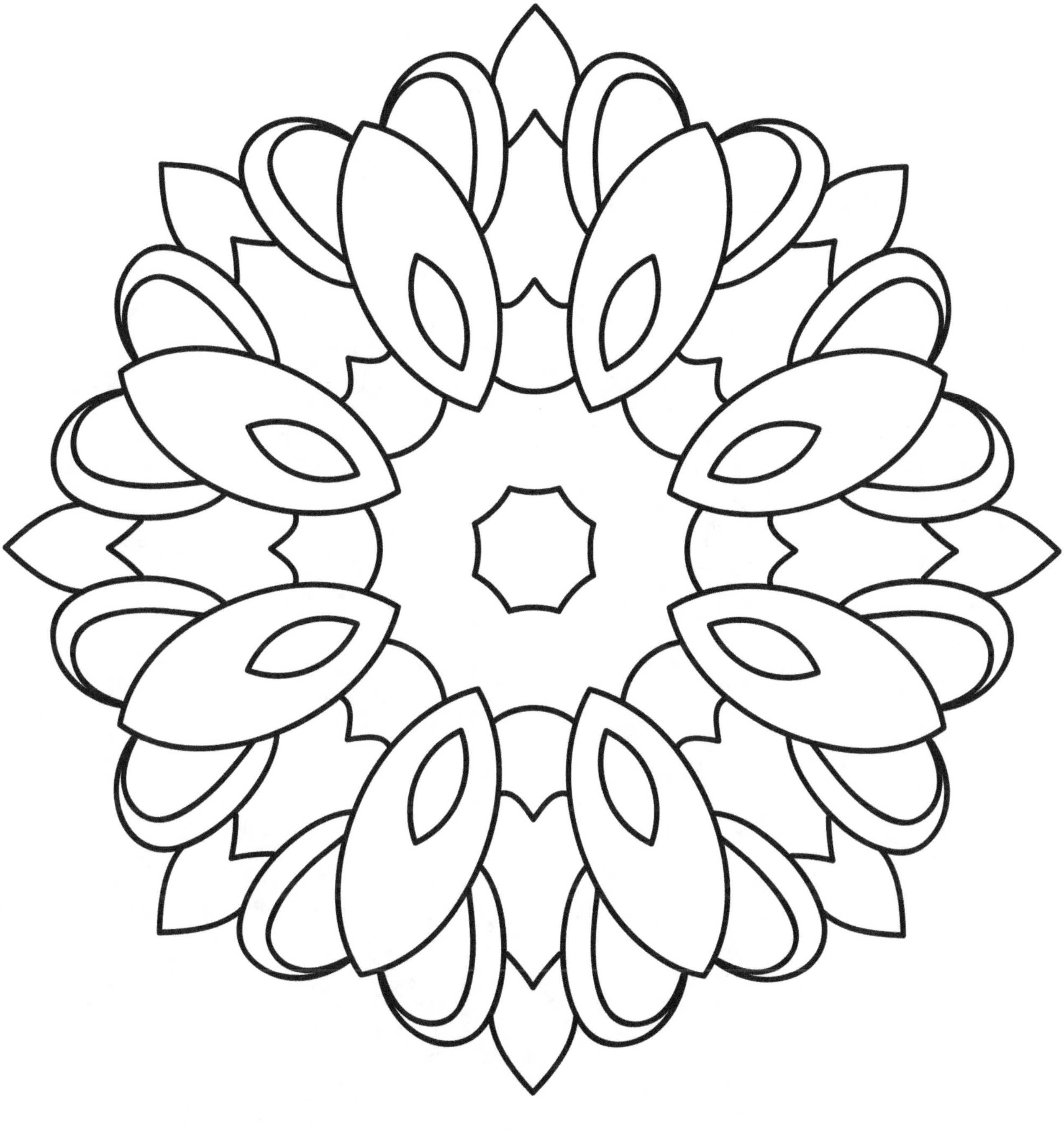

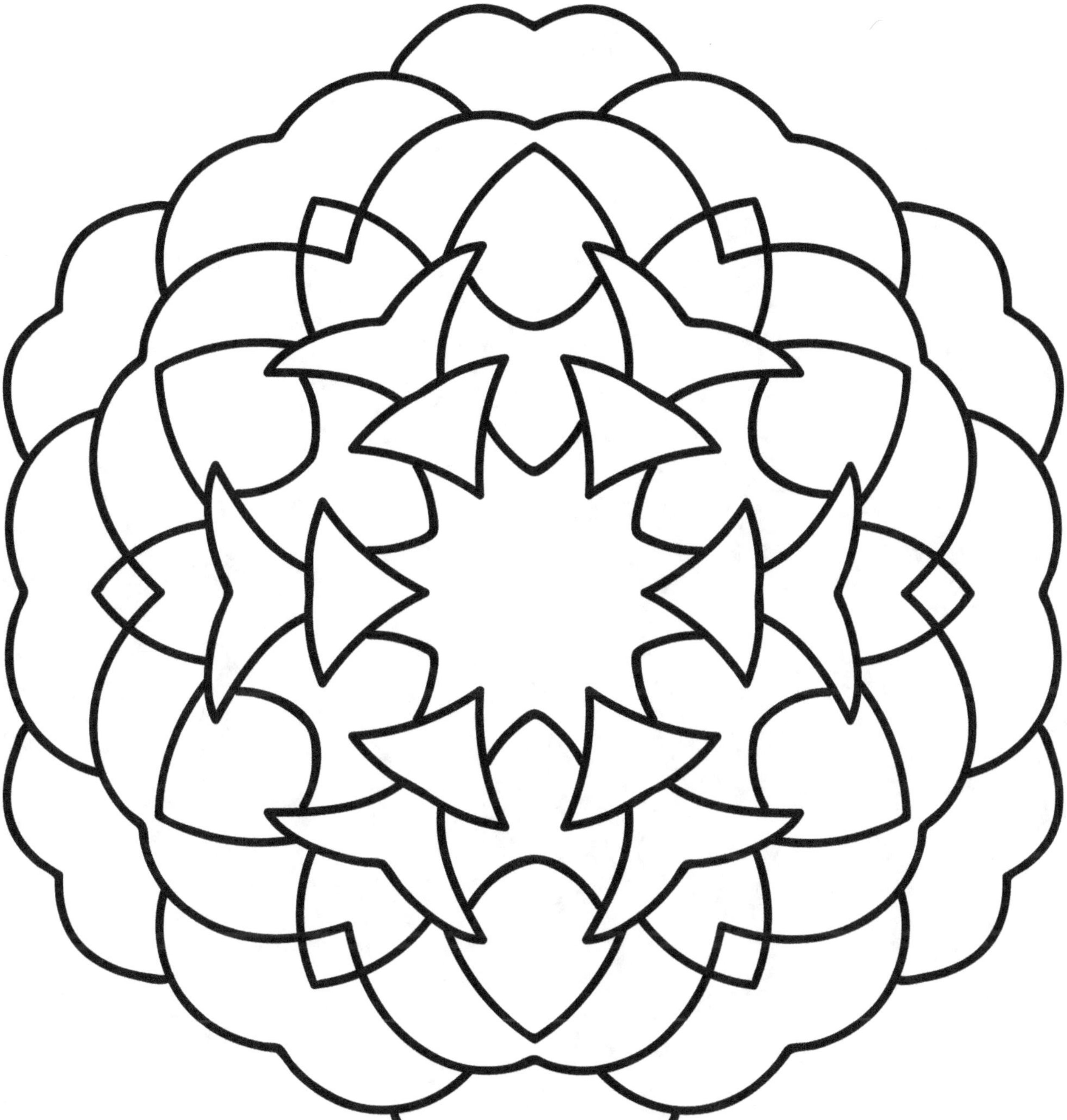

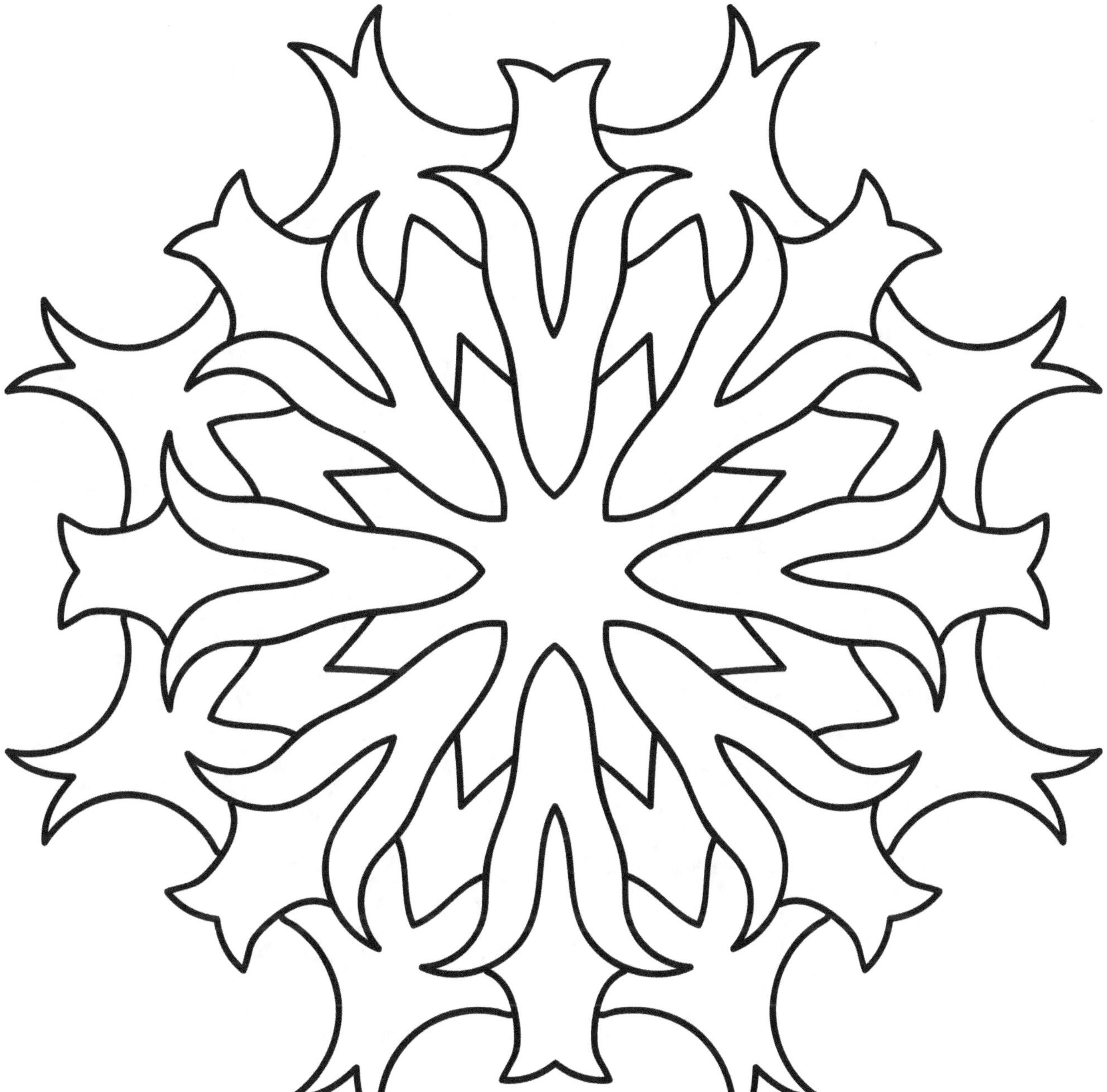

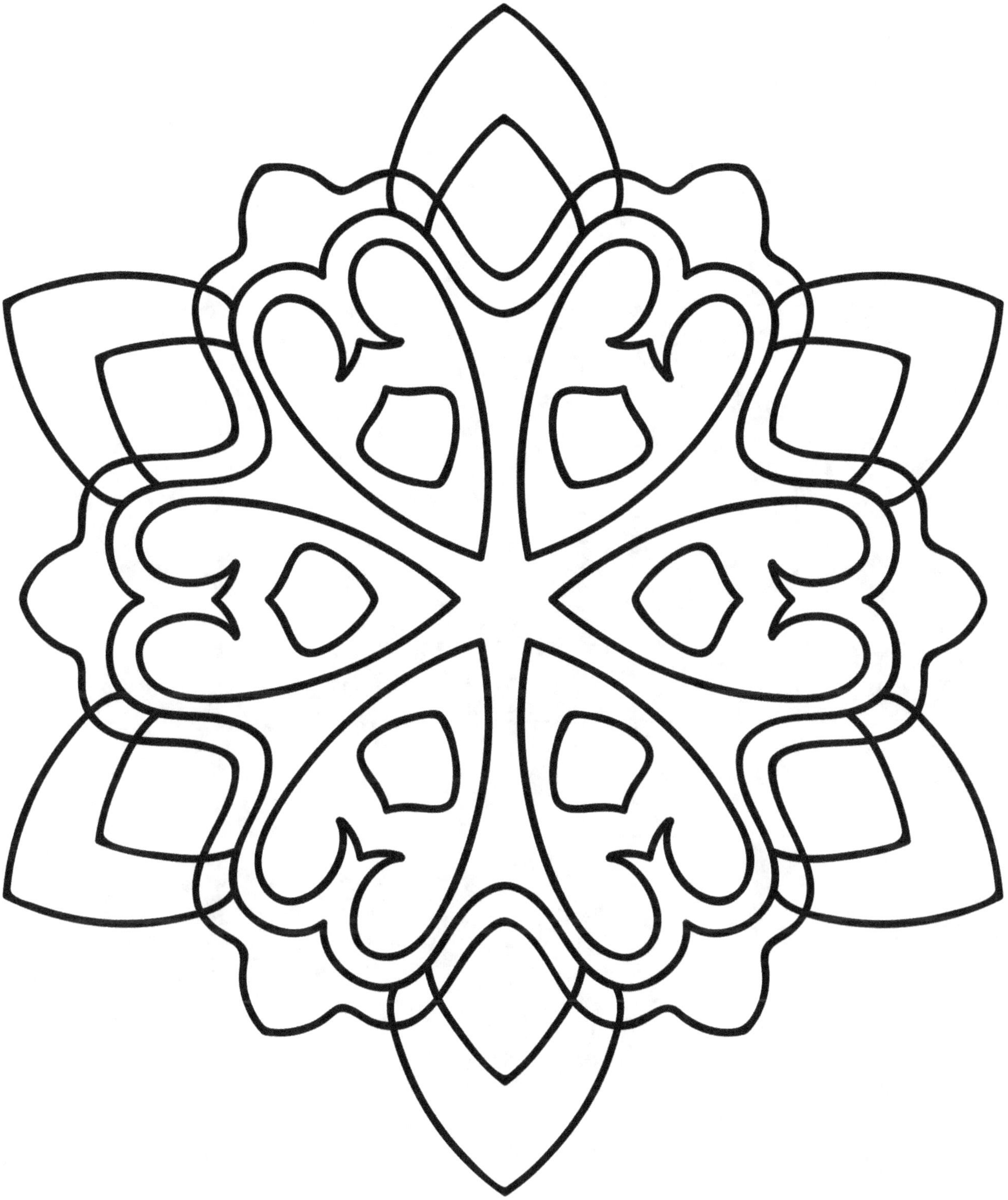

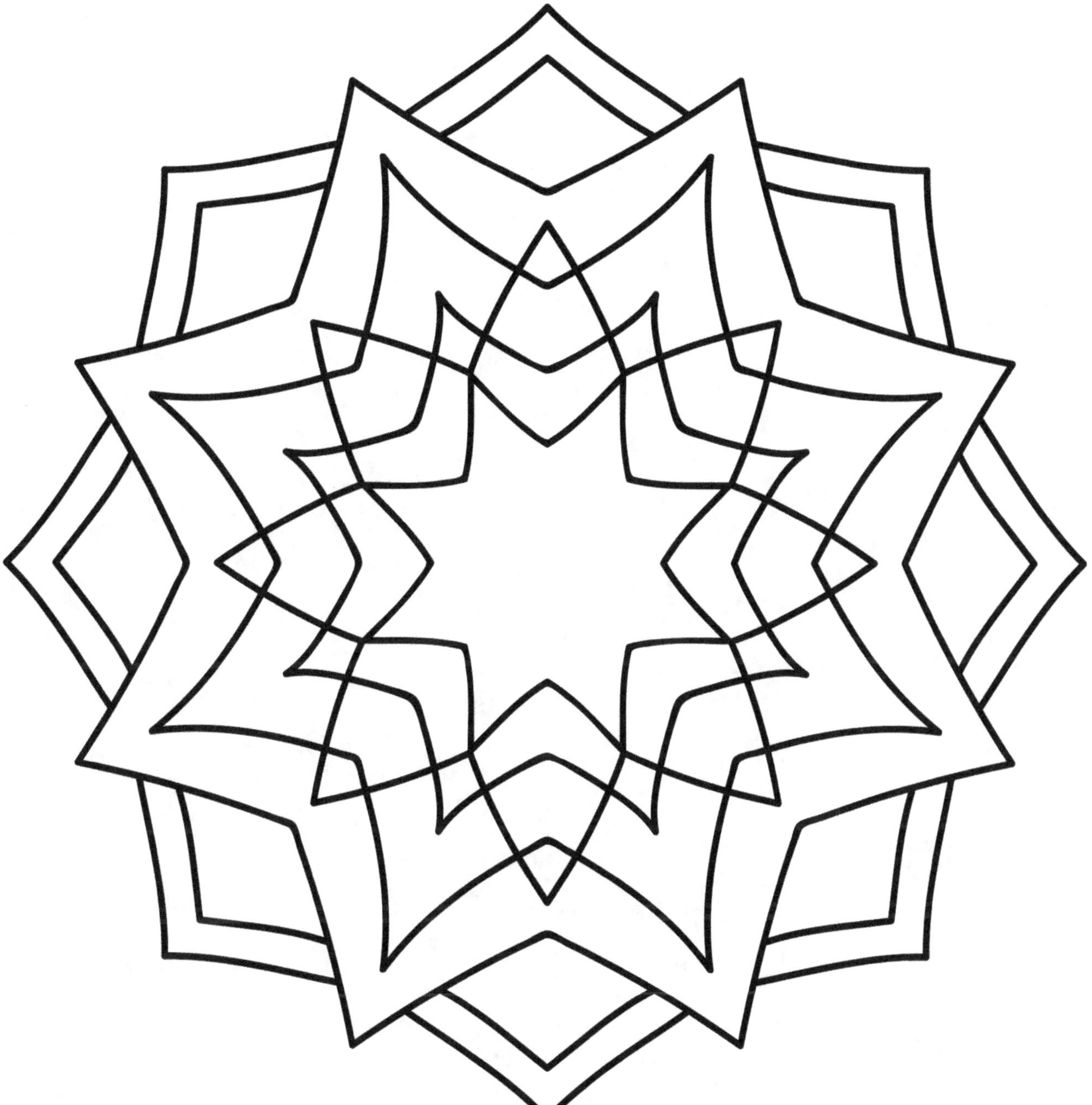

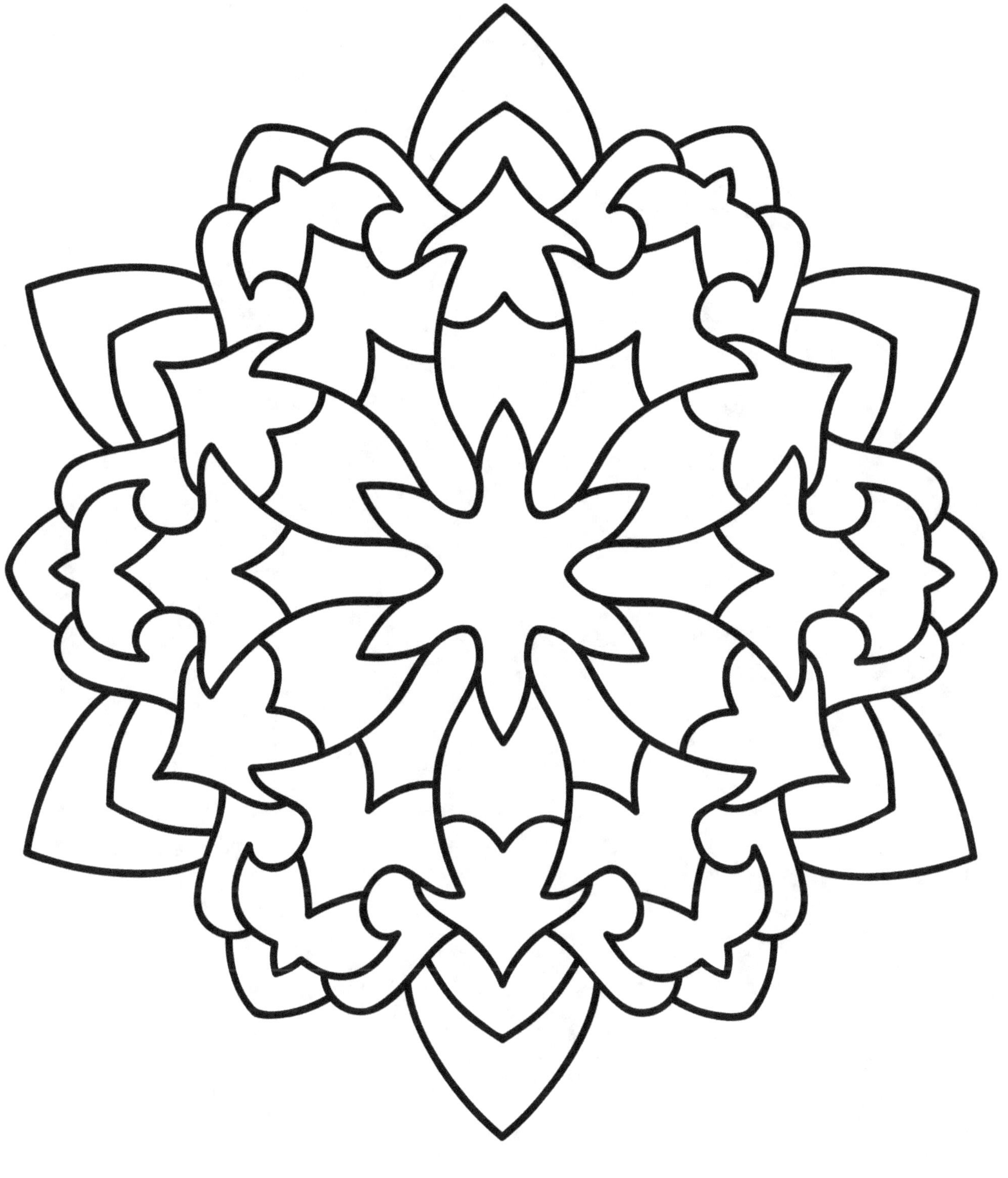

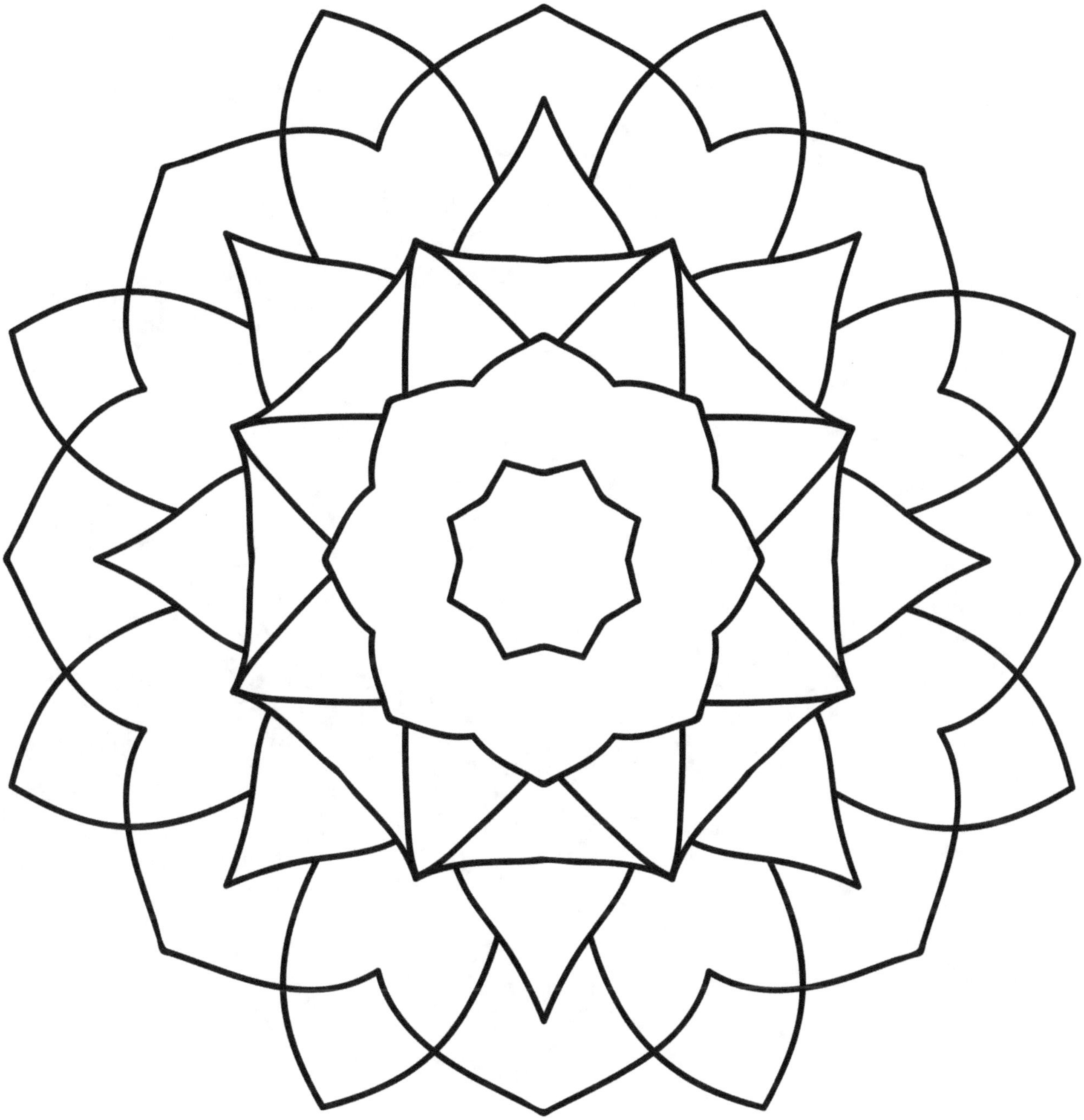

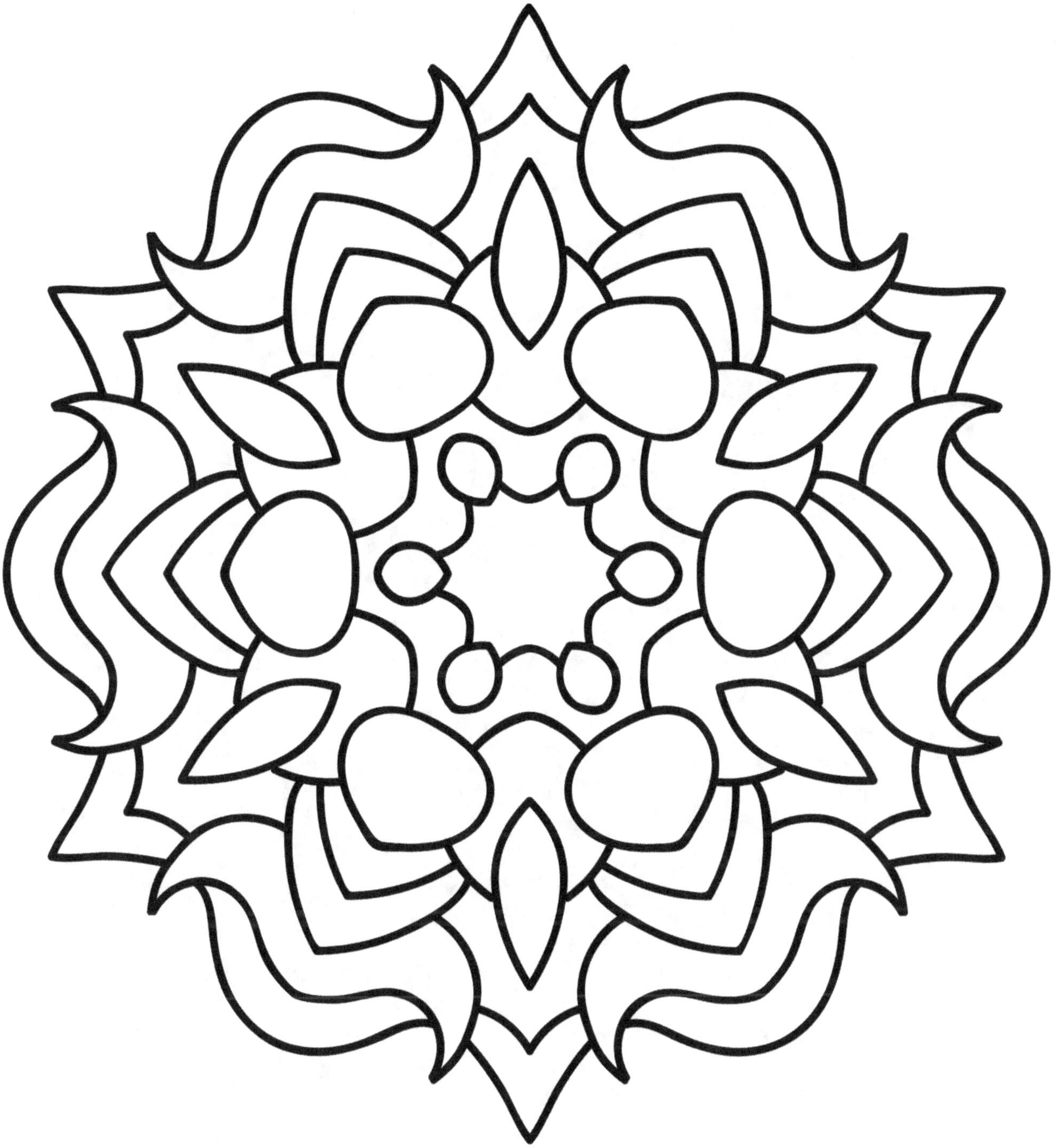

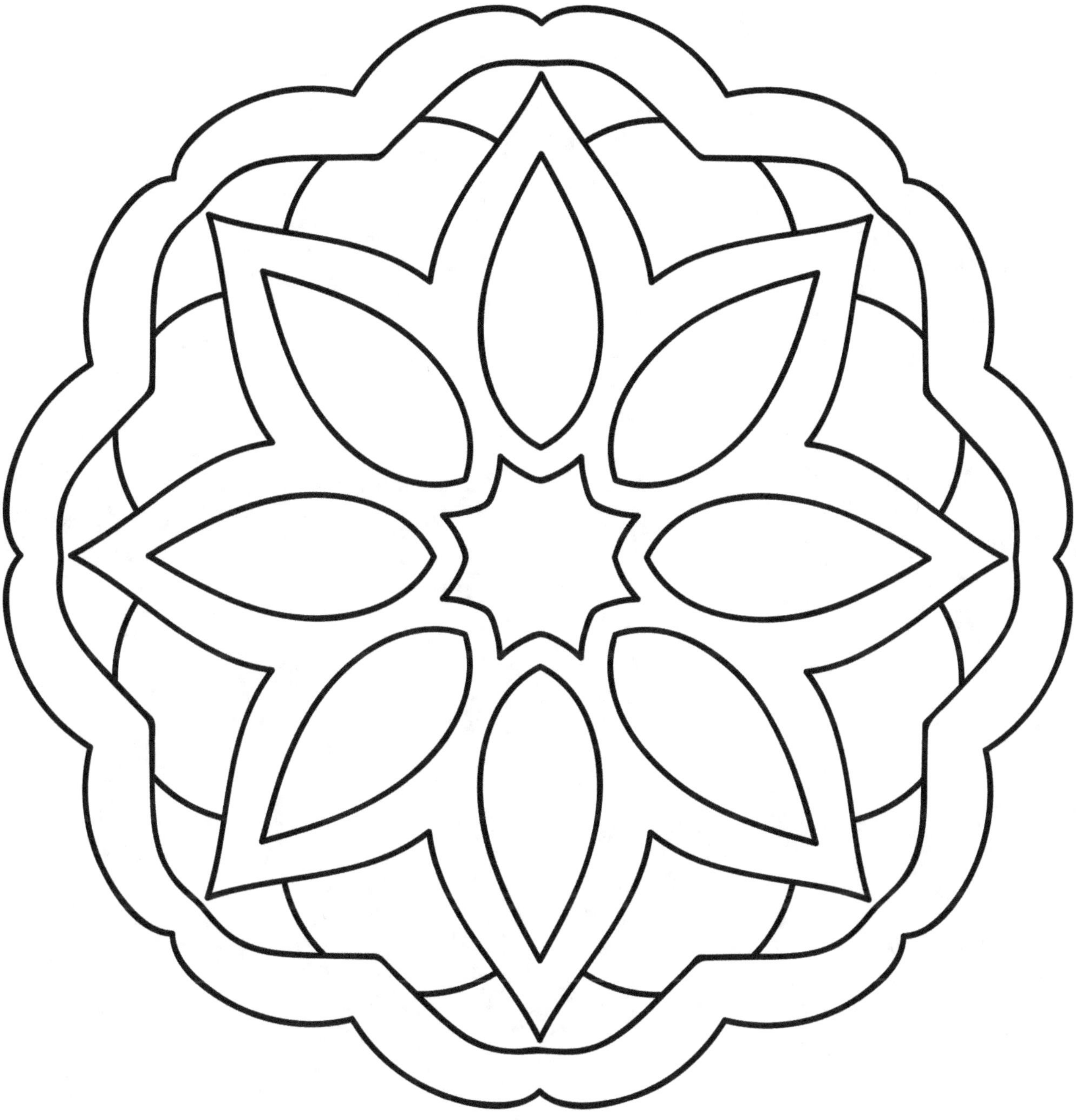

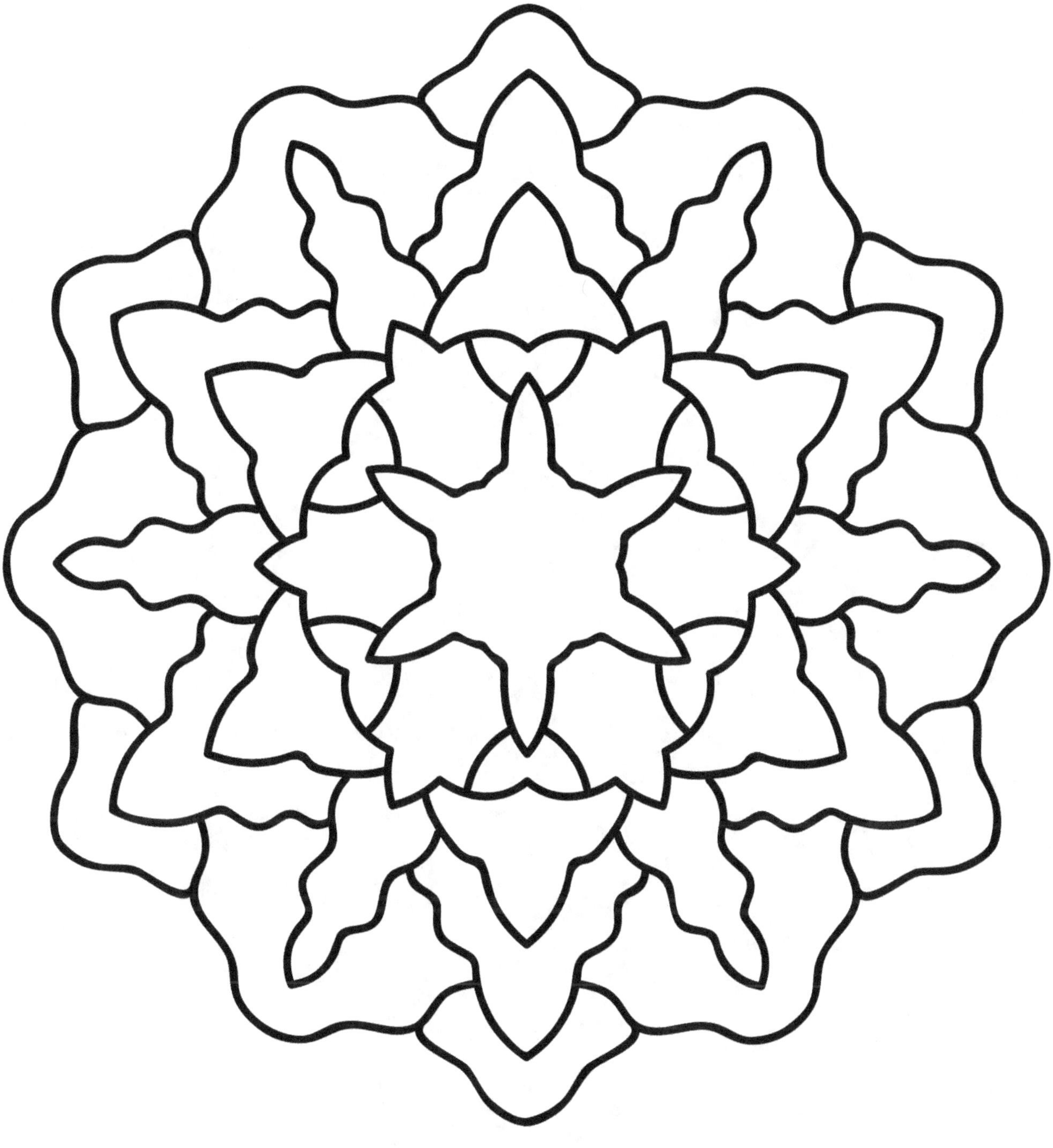

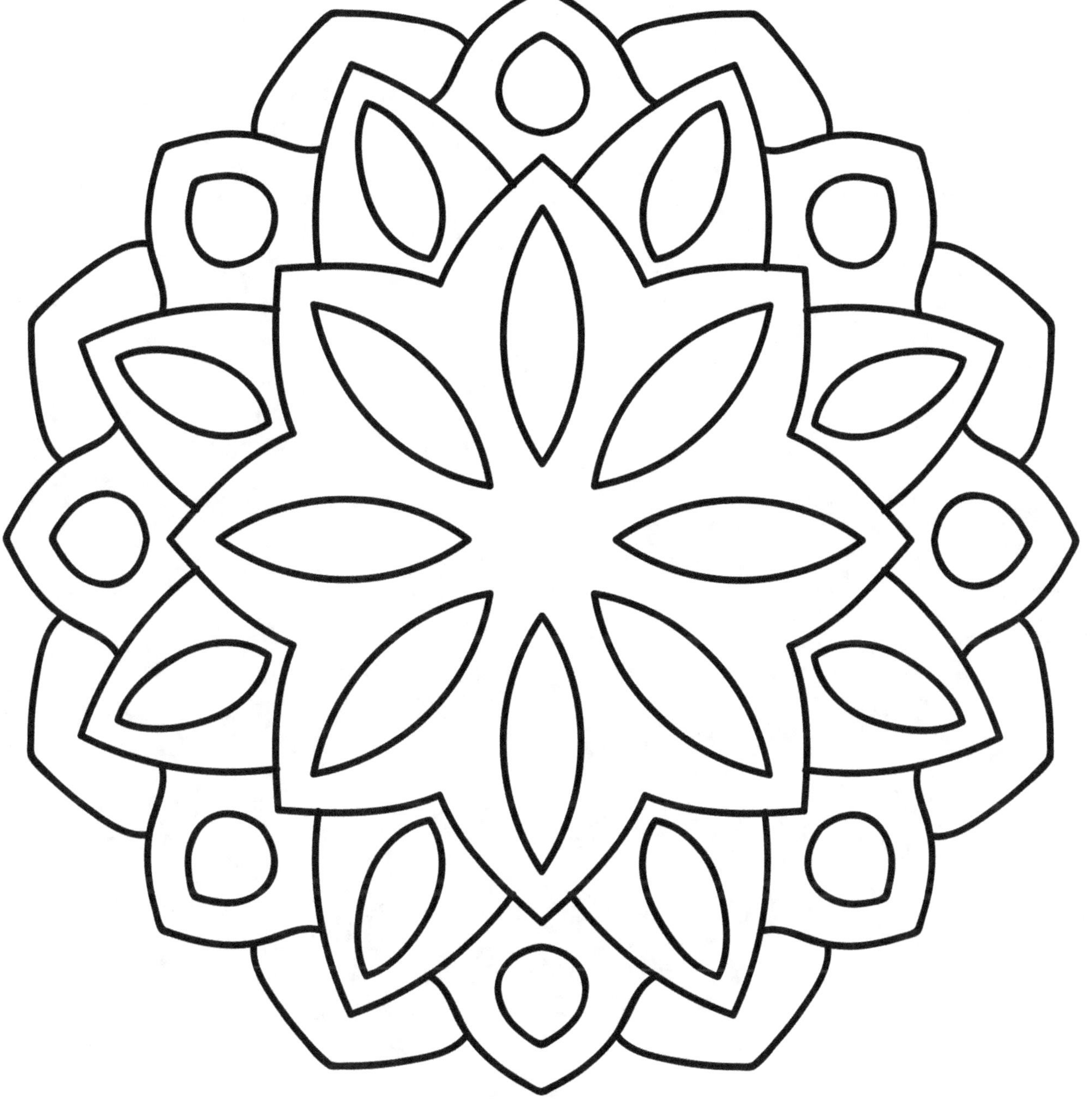

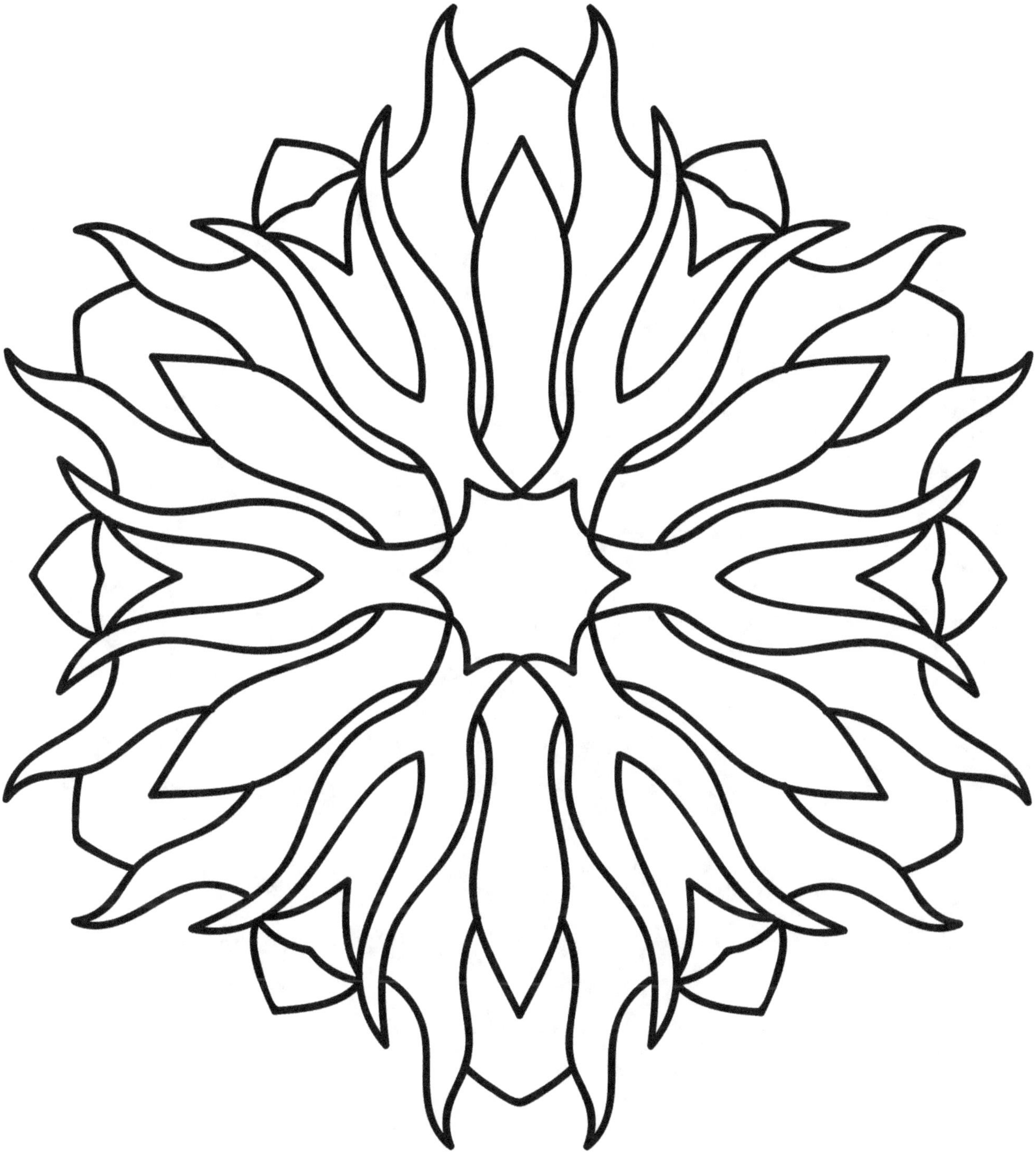

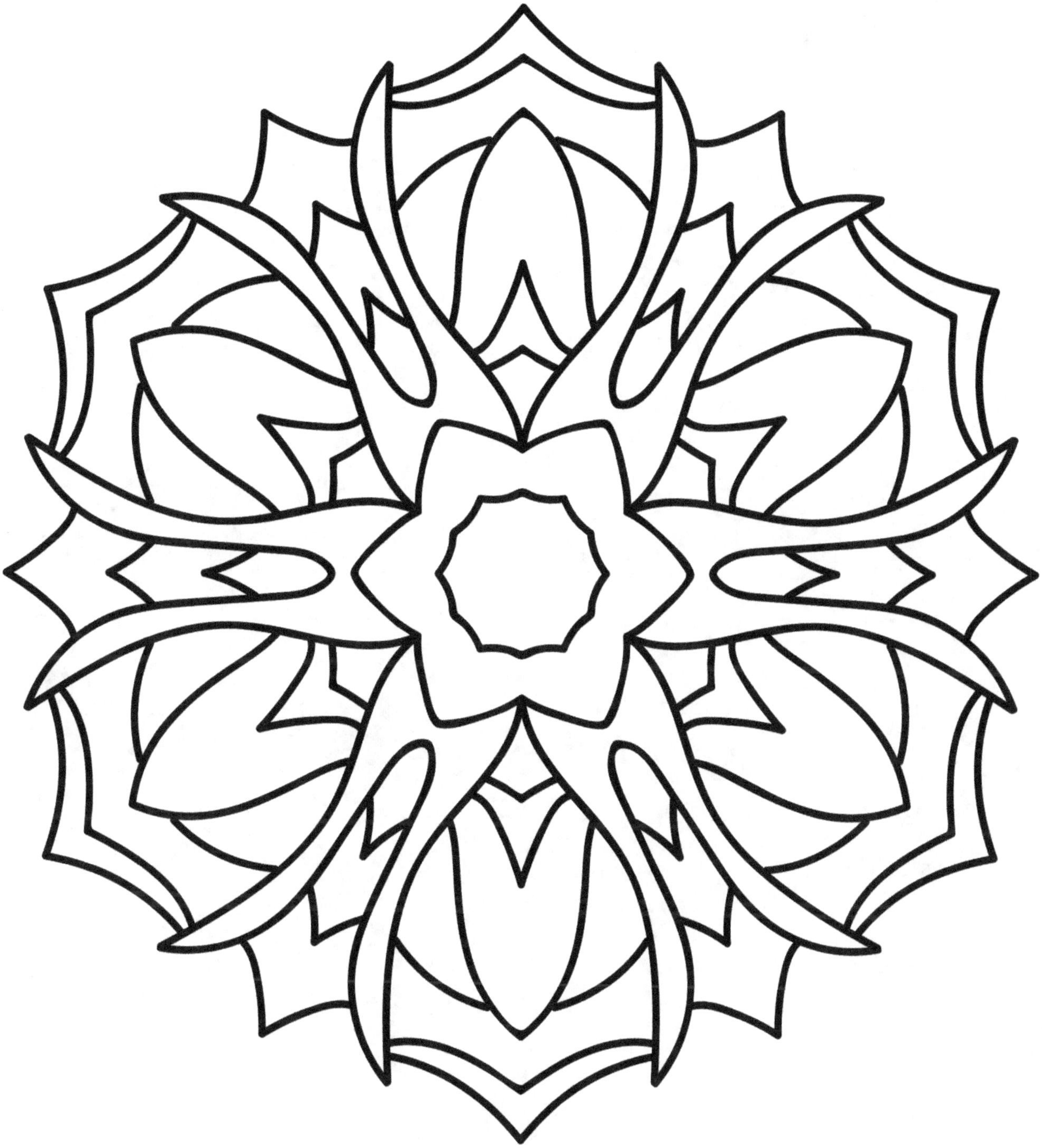

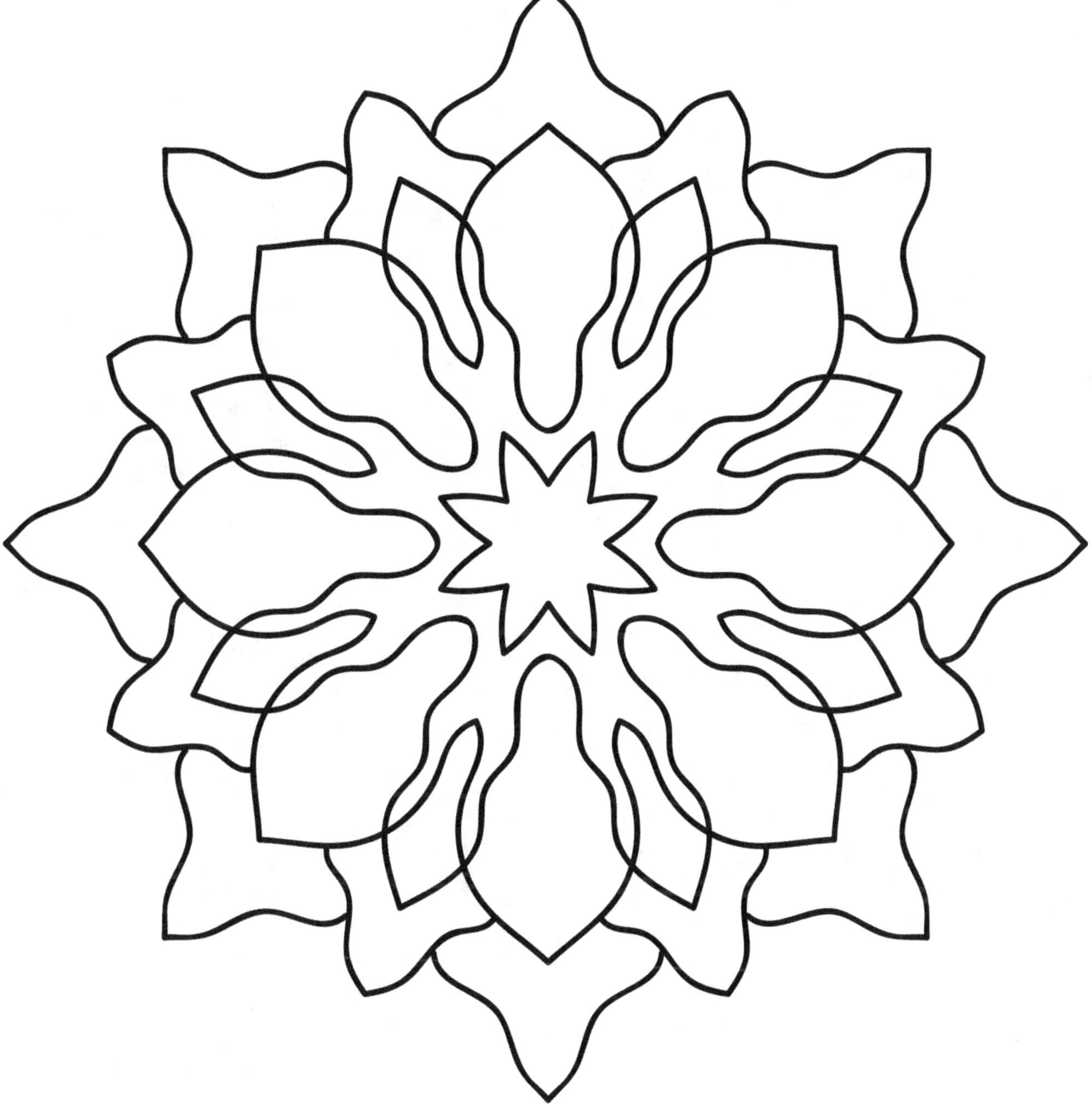

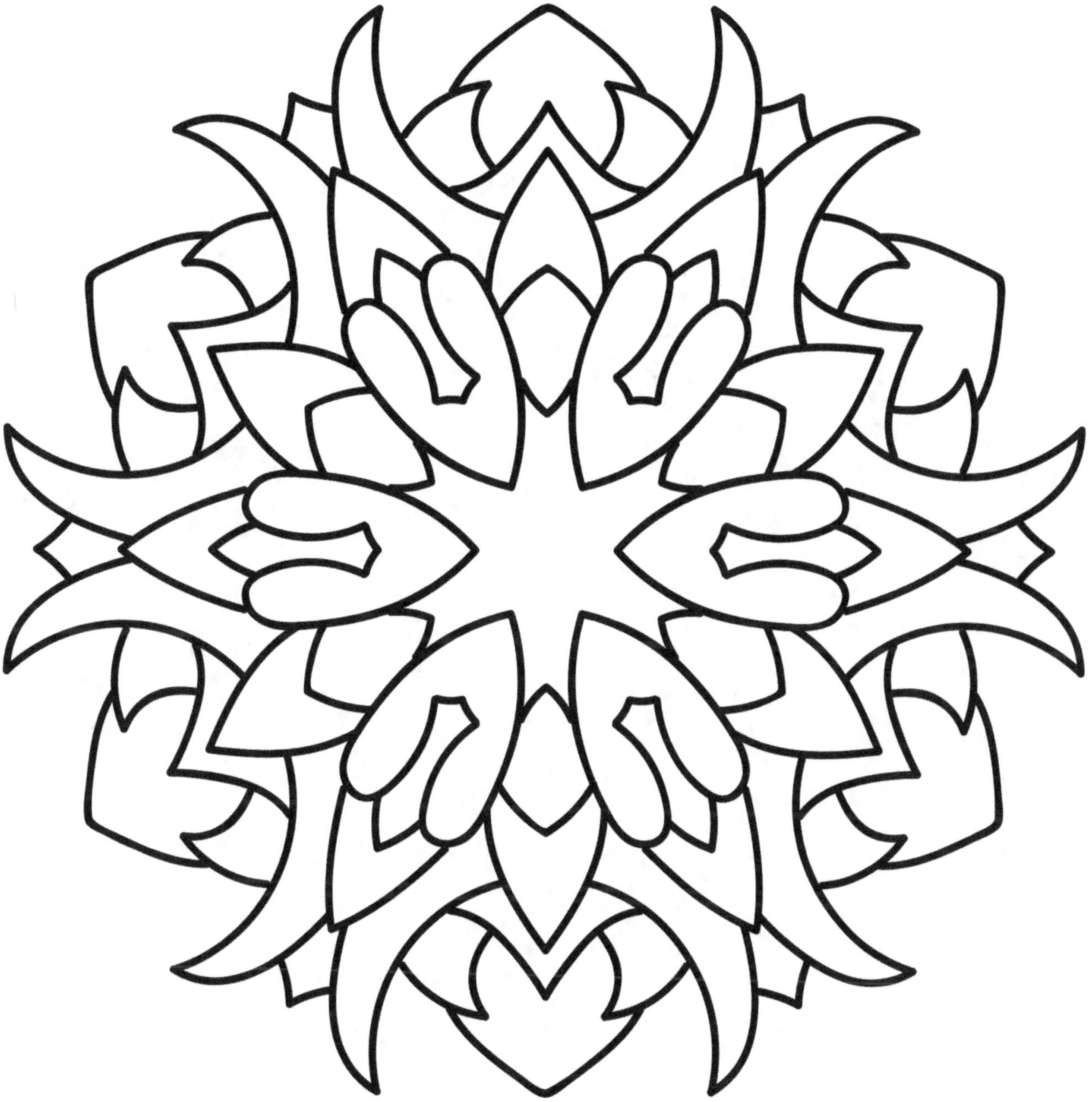

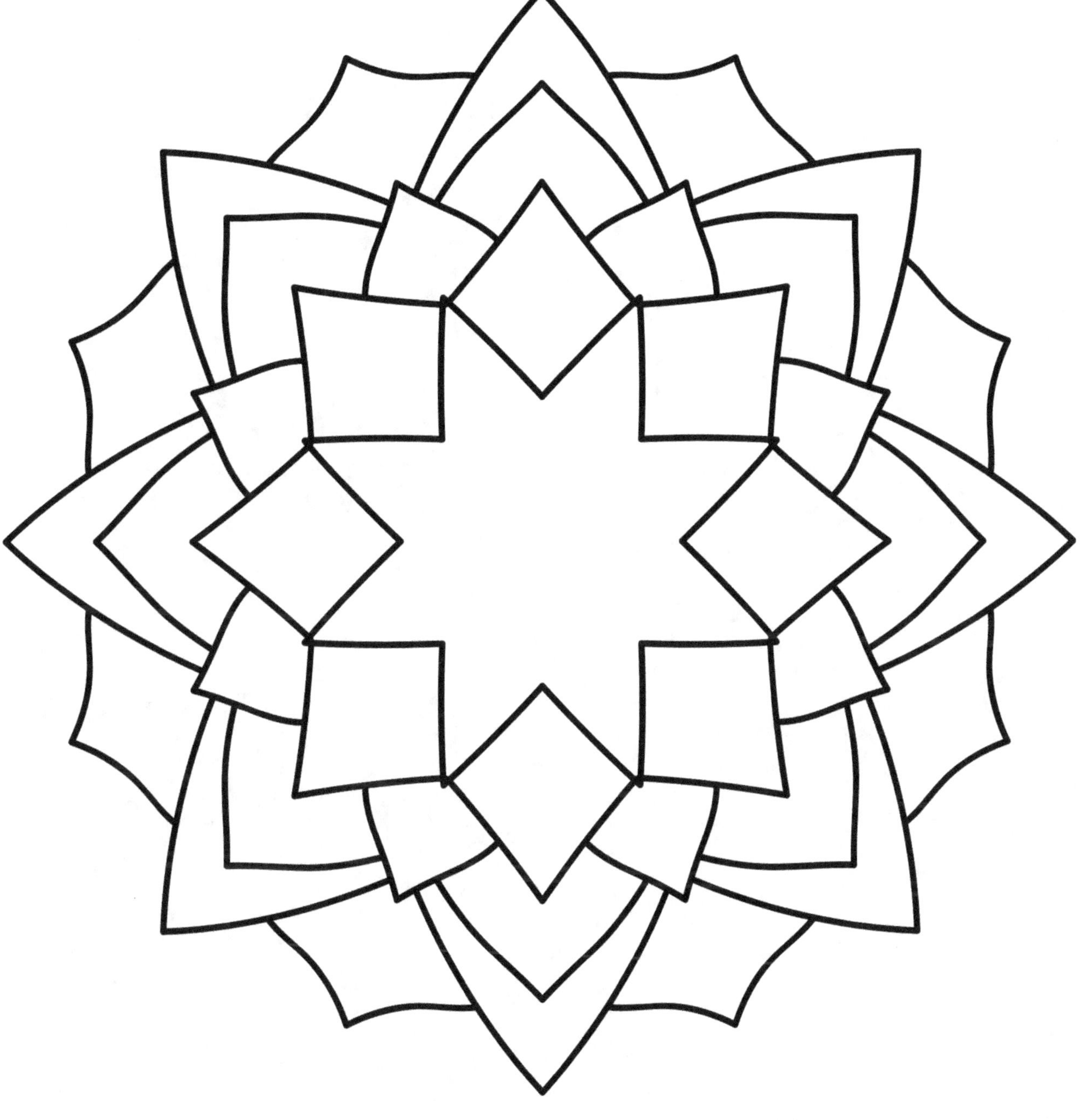

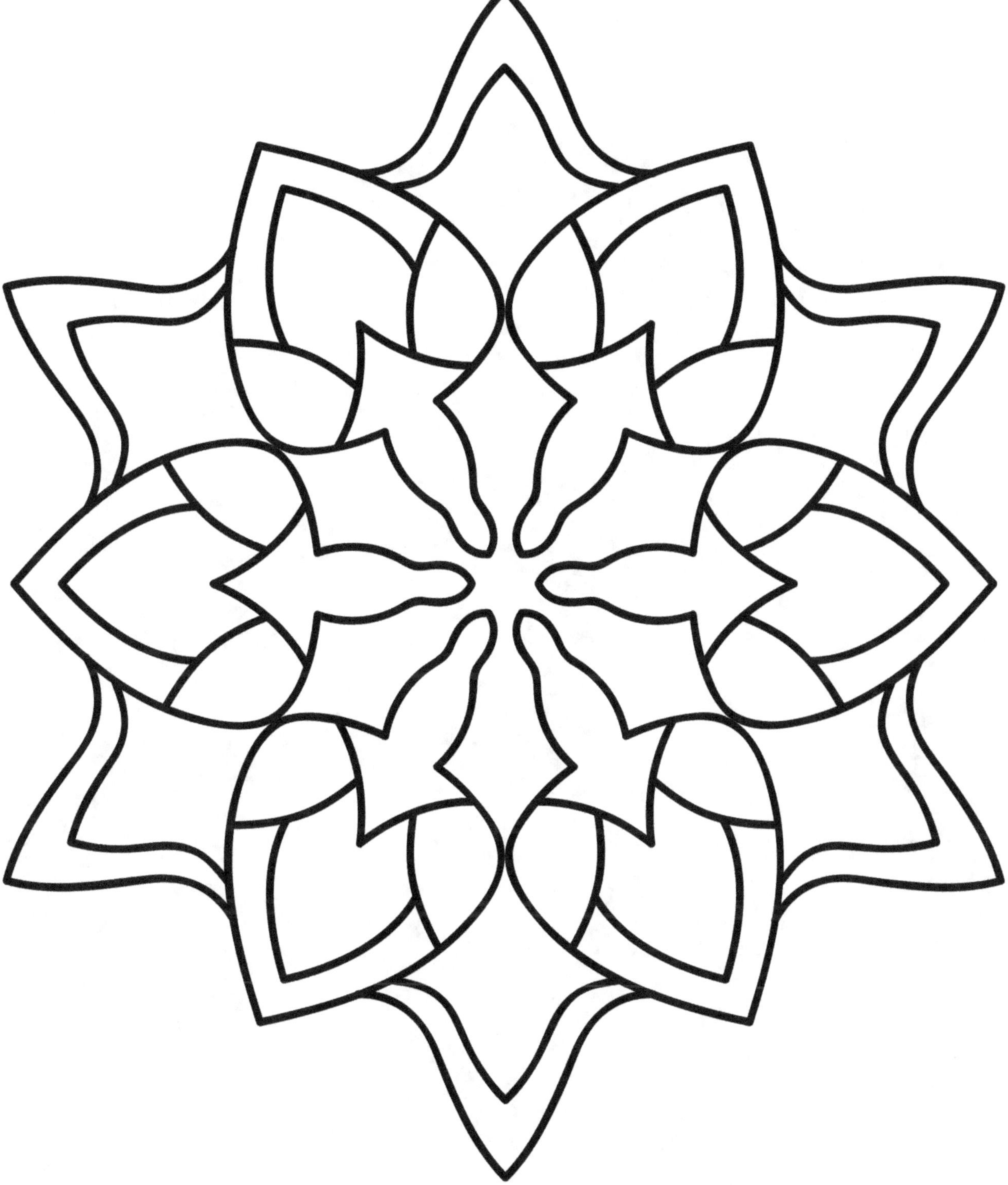

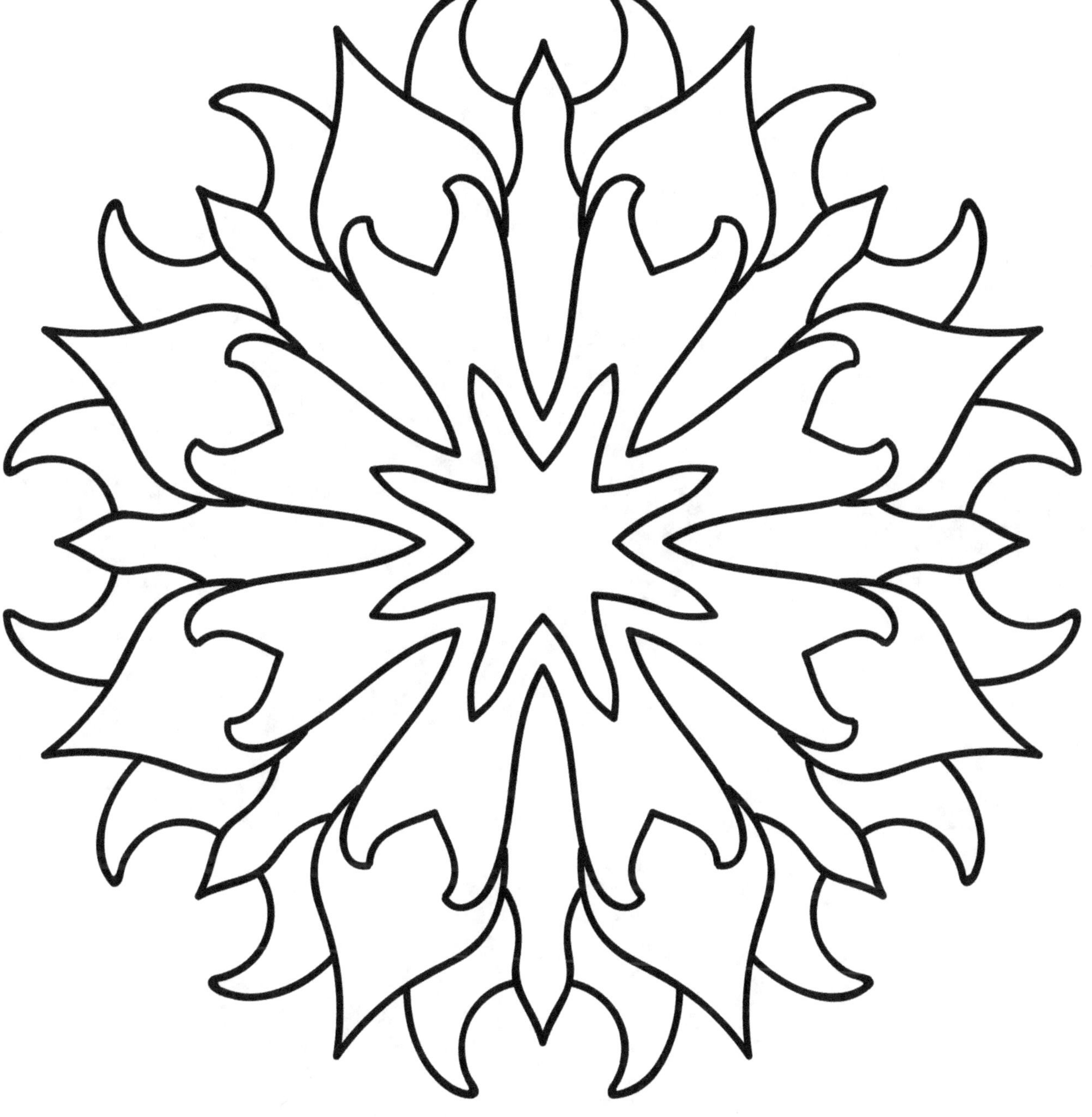

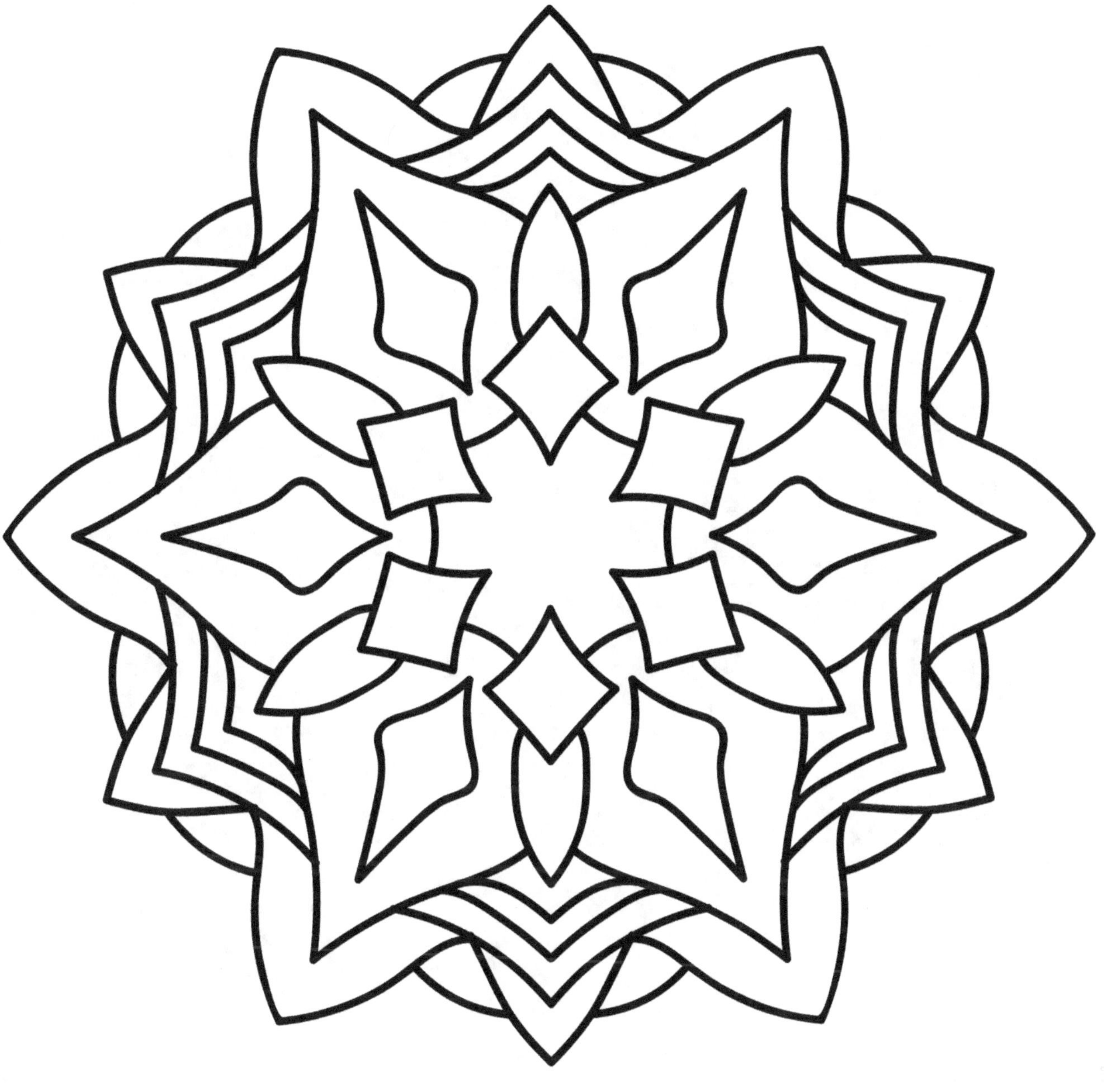

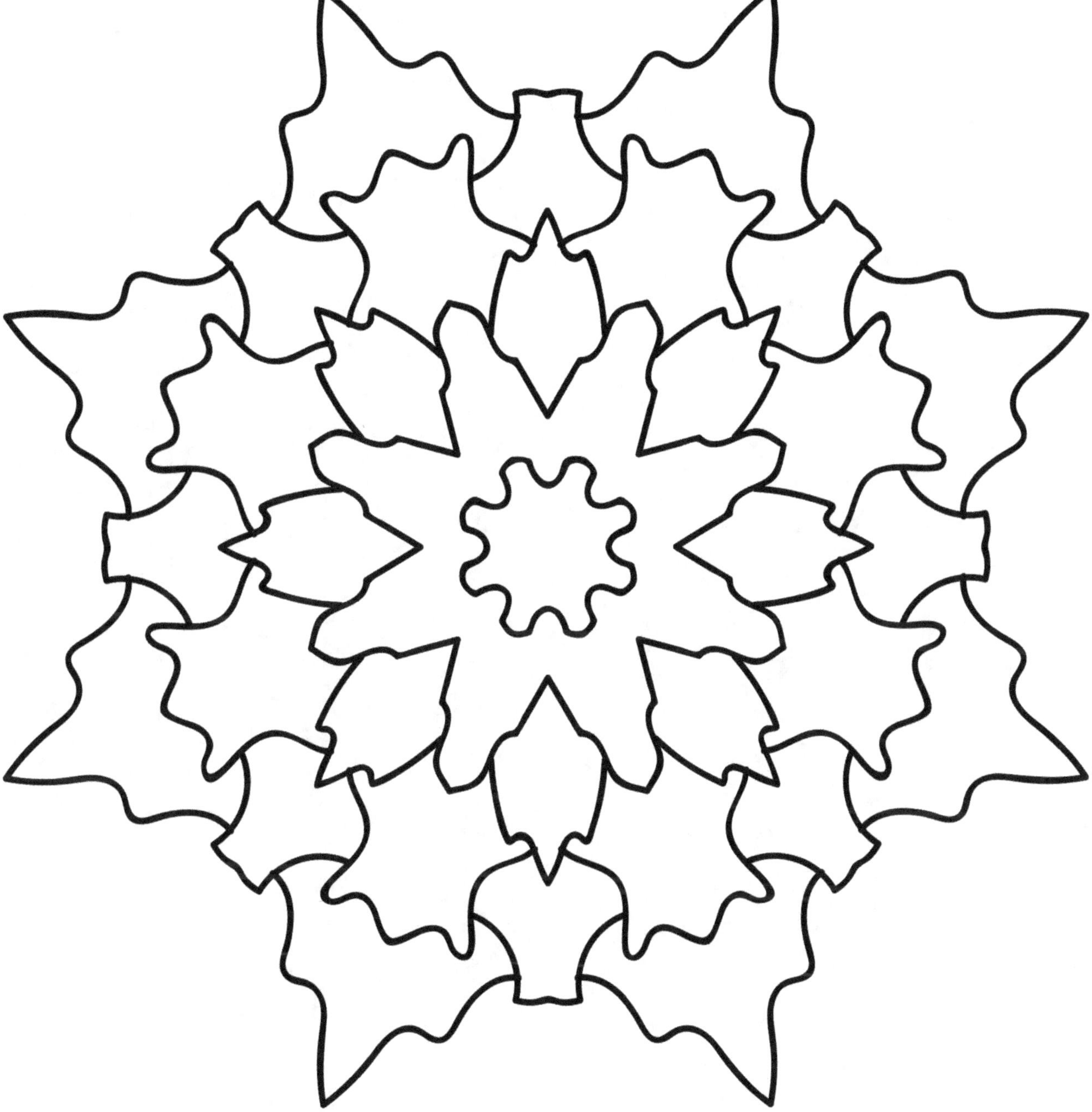

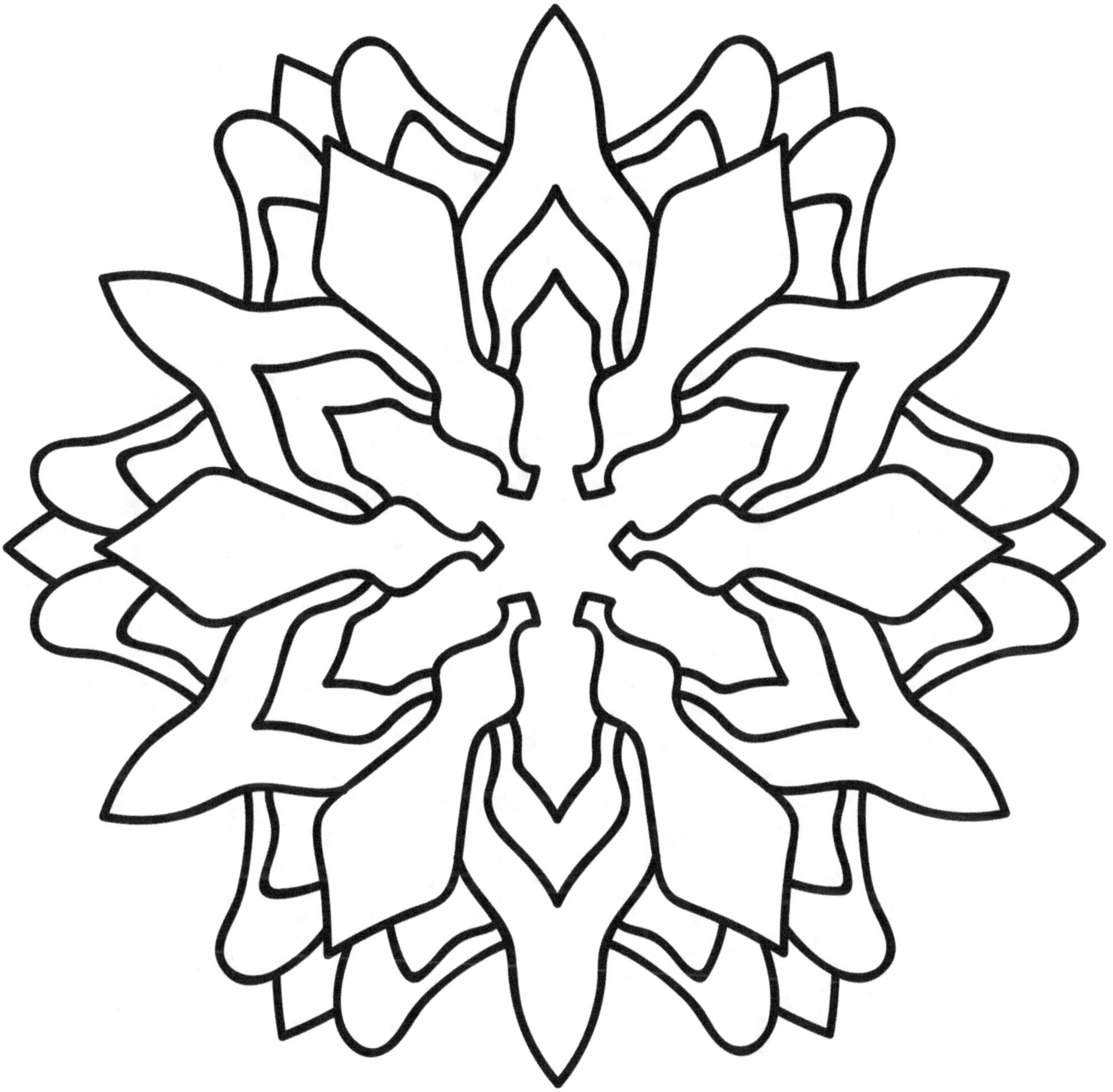

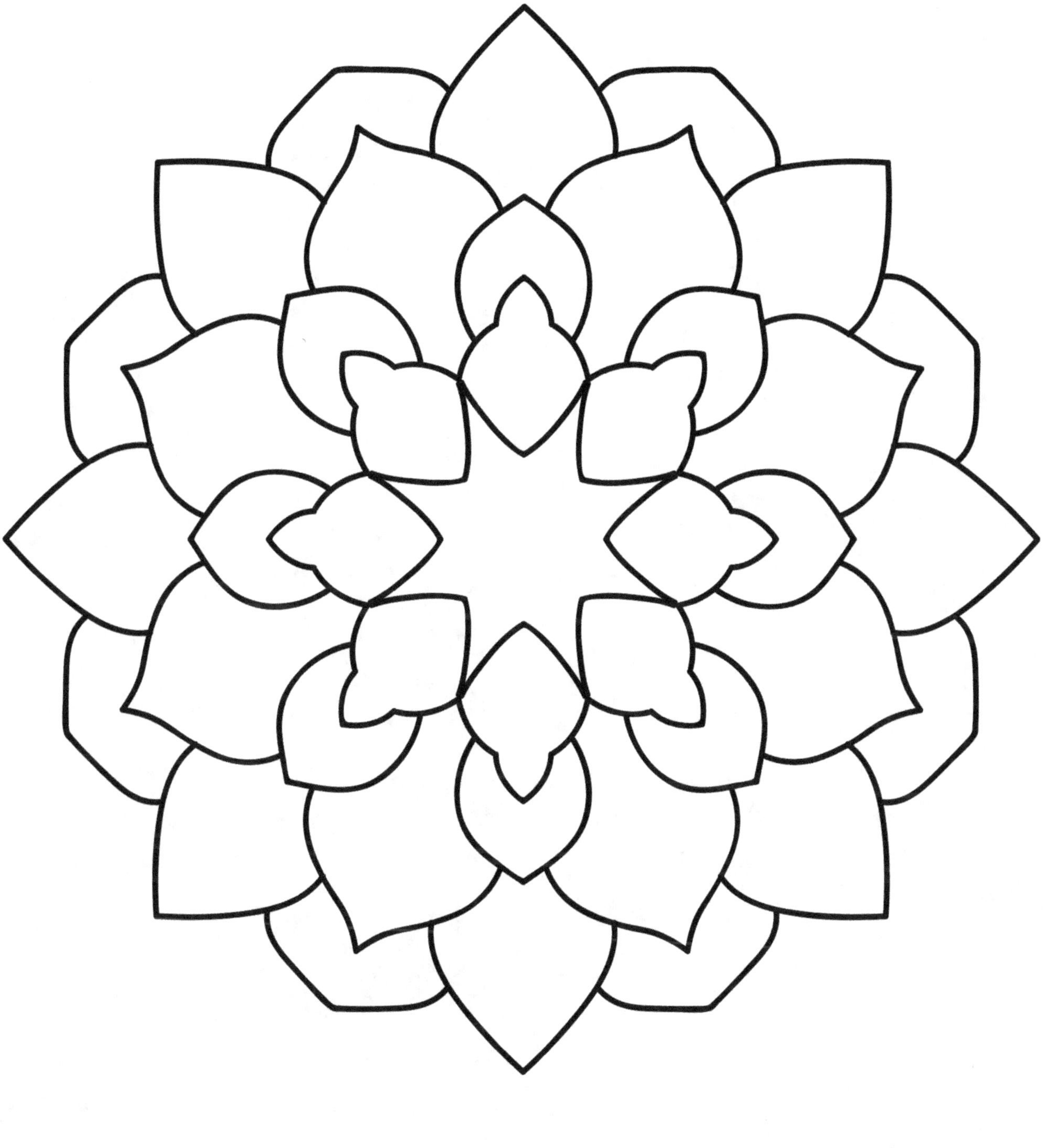

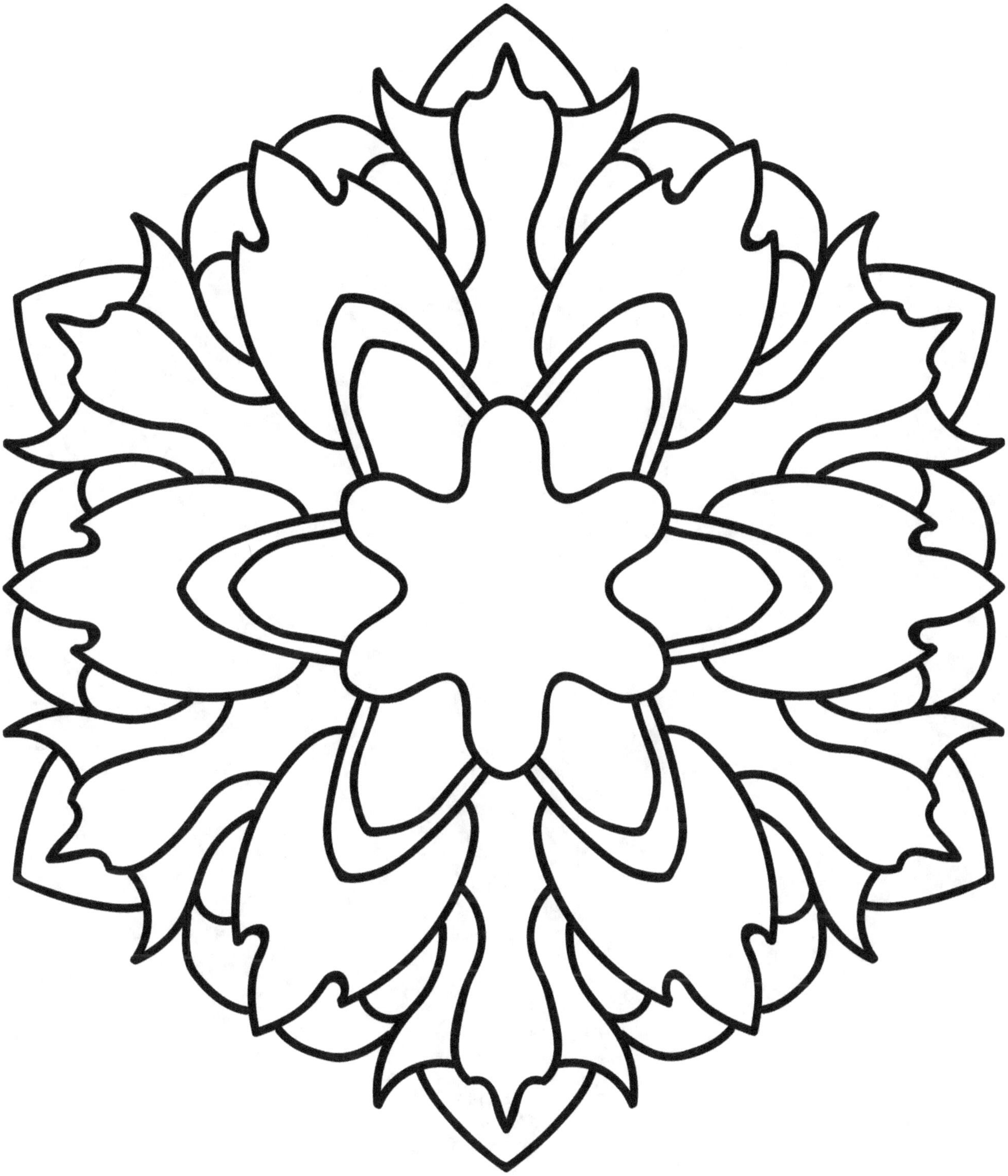

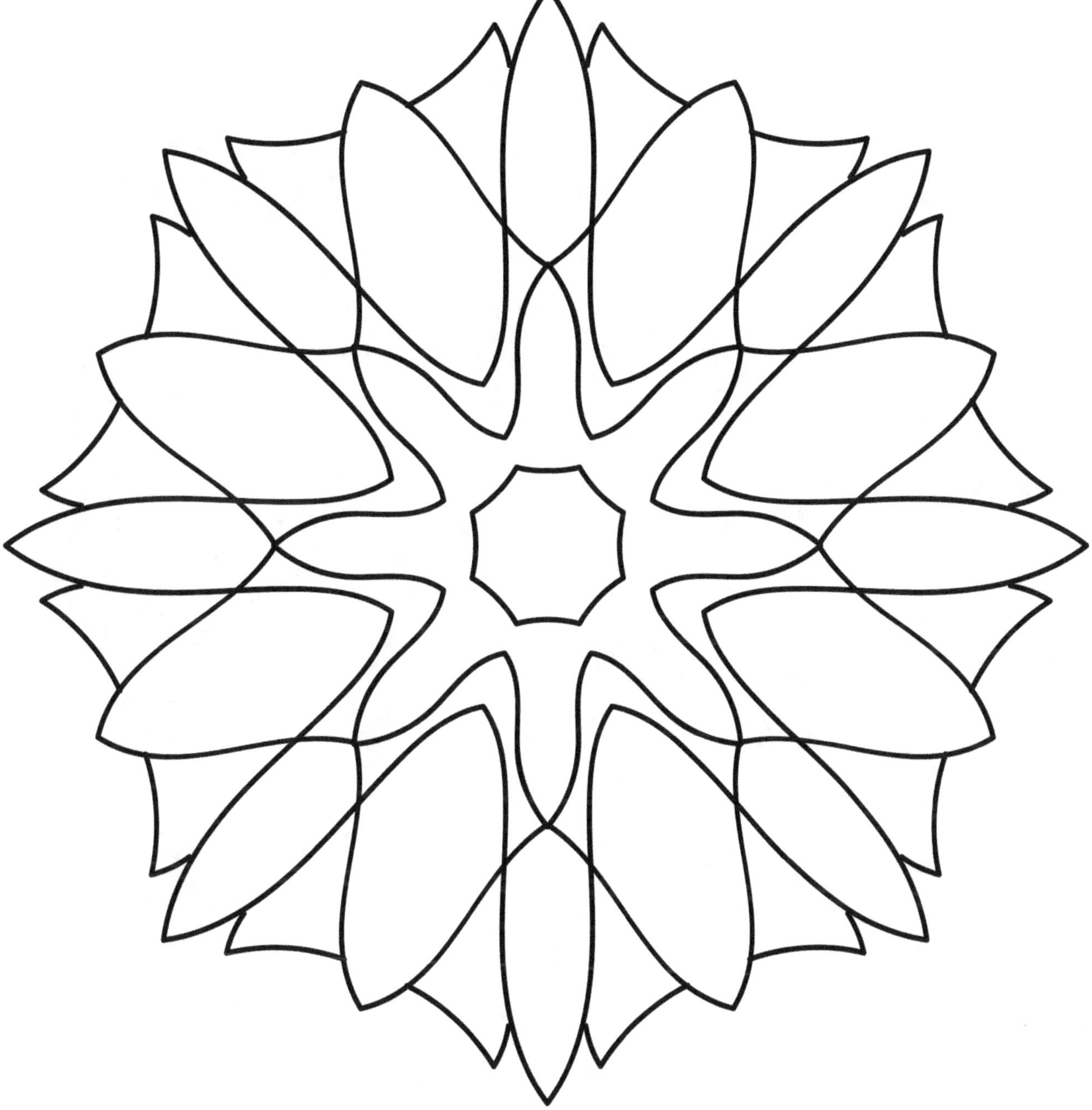

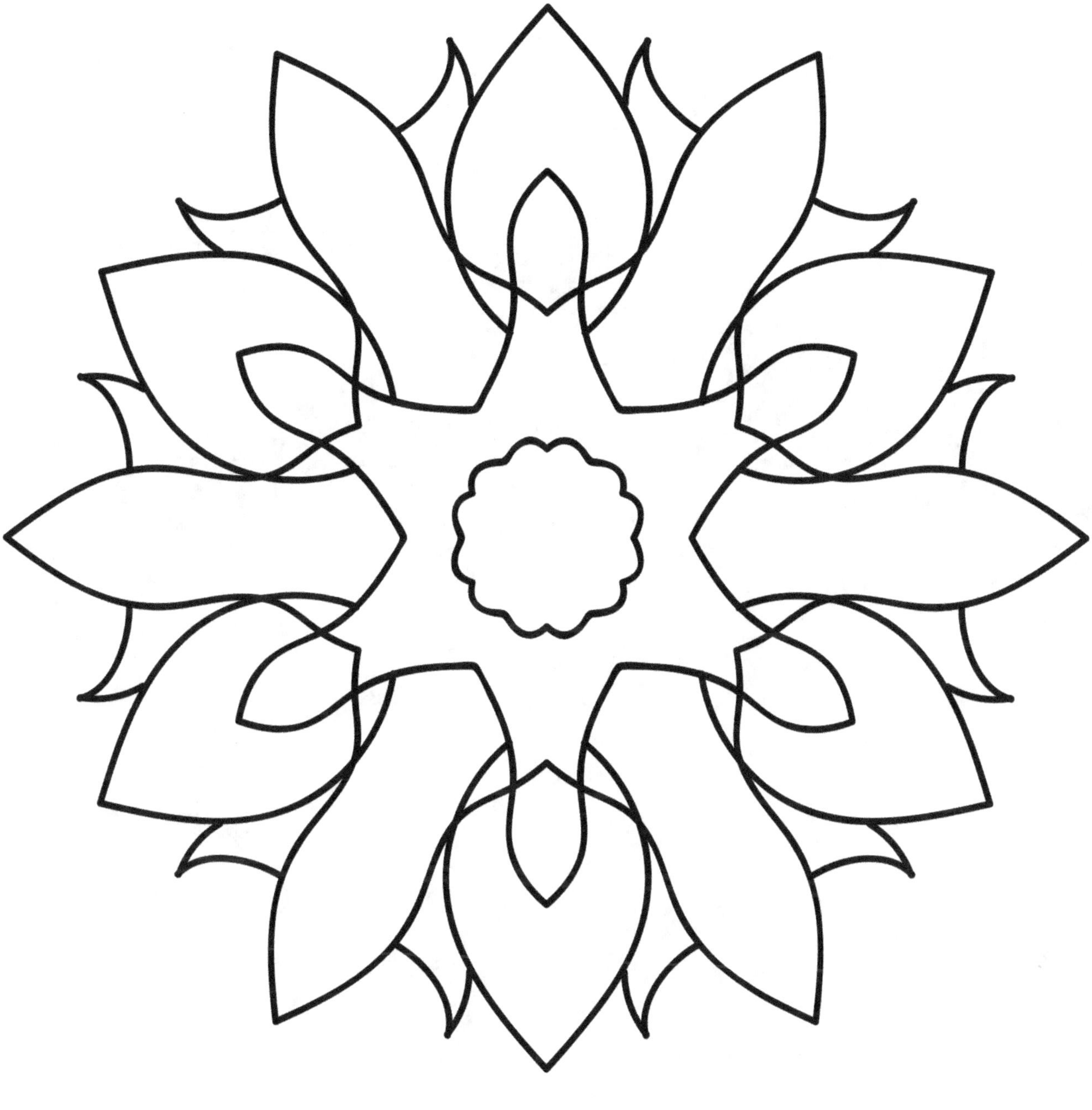

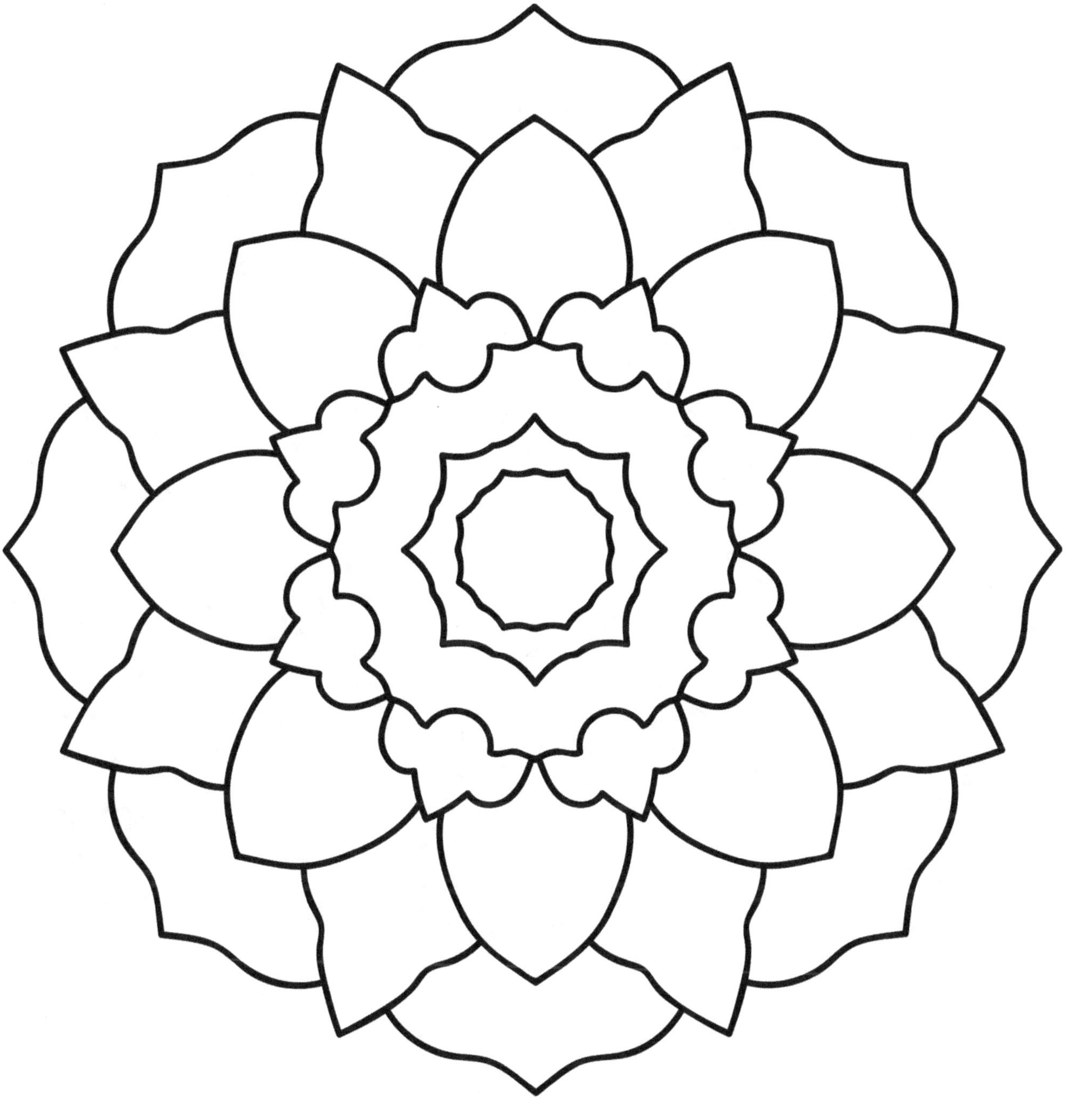

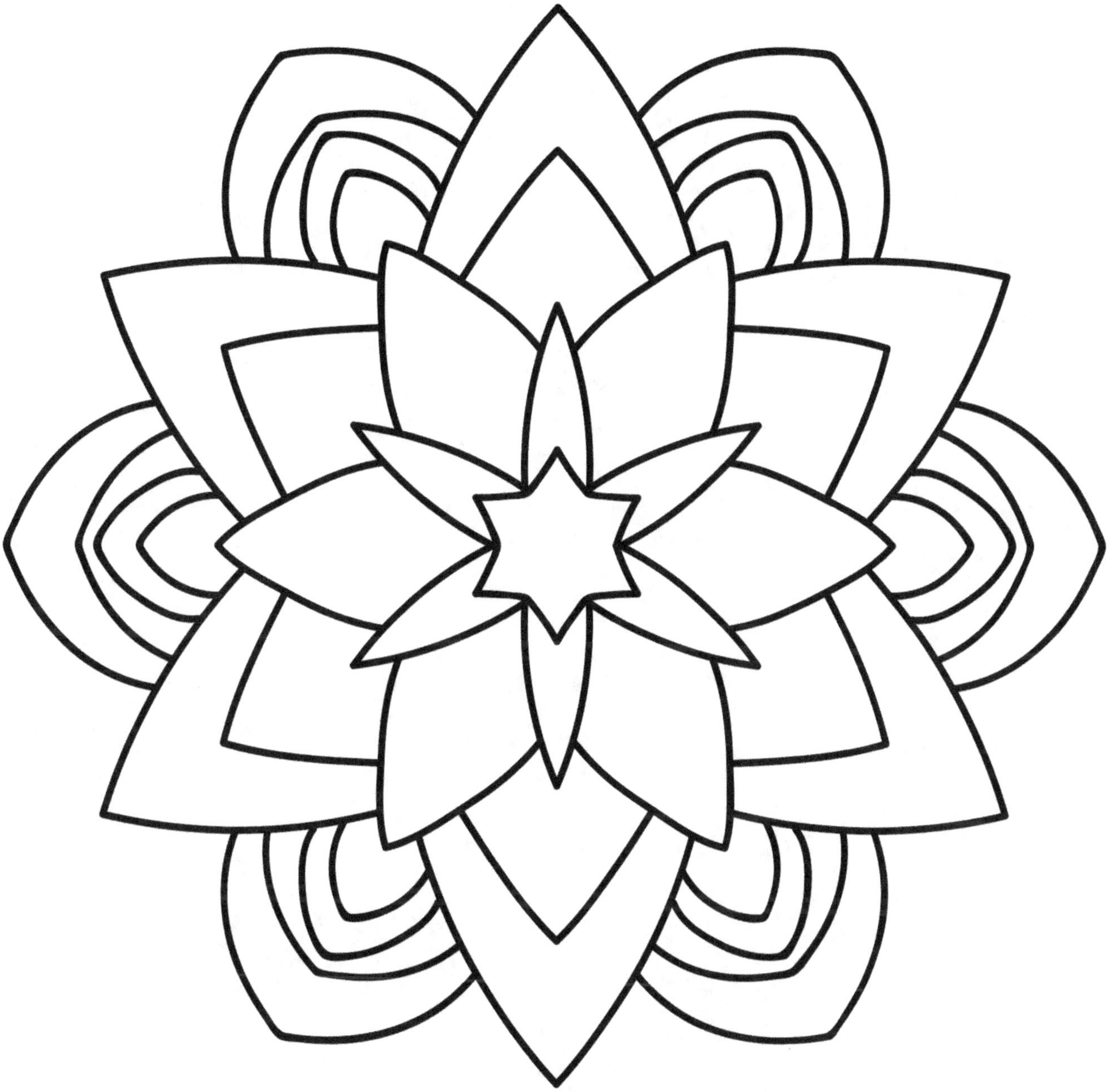

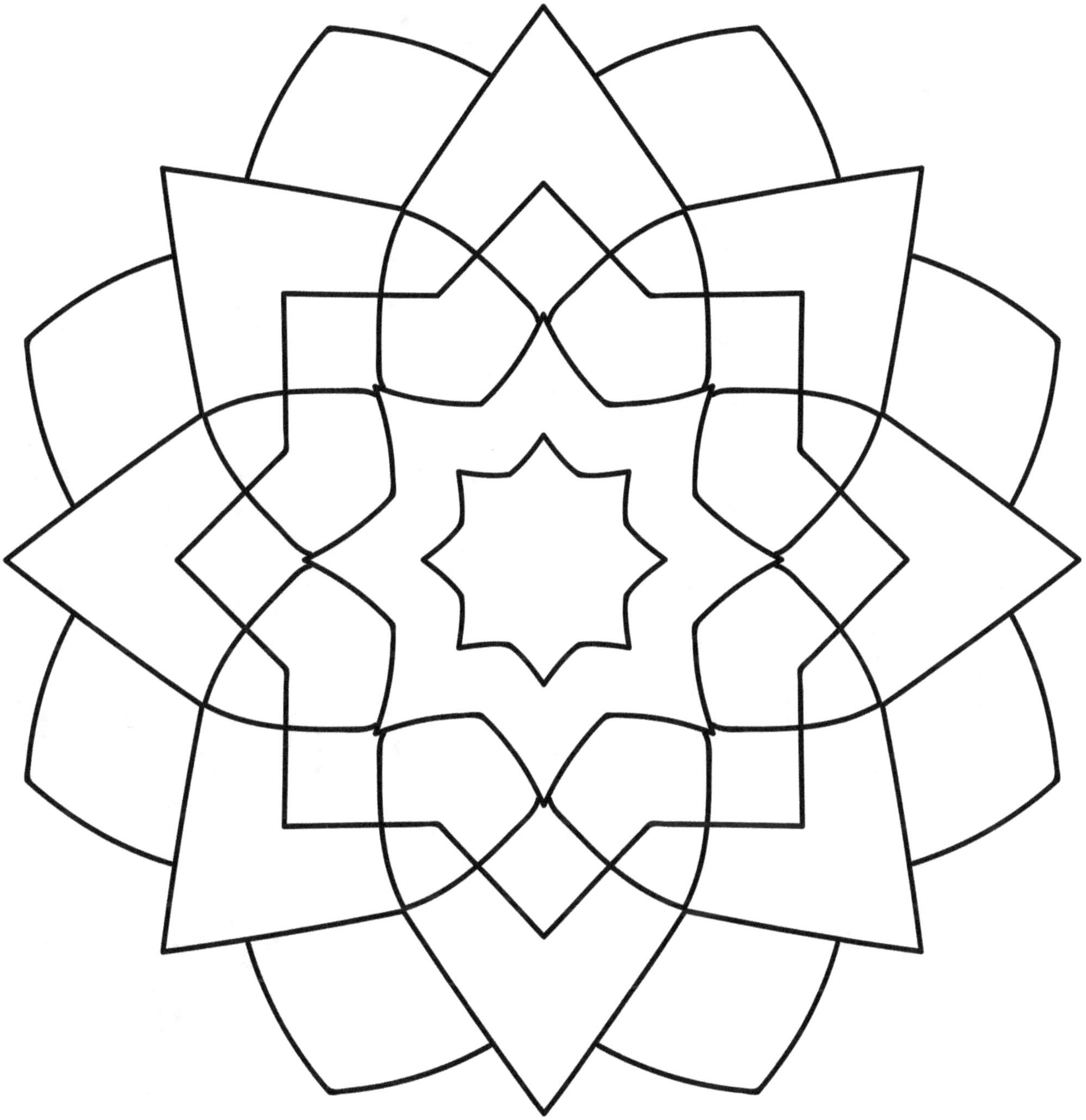

www.ingramcontent.com/pod-product-compliance
Lightning Source LLC
Chambersburg PA
CBHW081557170526
45166CB00009B/2731
9781522719786